# Diagonal (or On-Point) Set

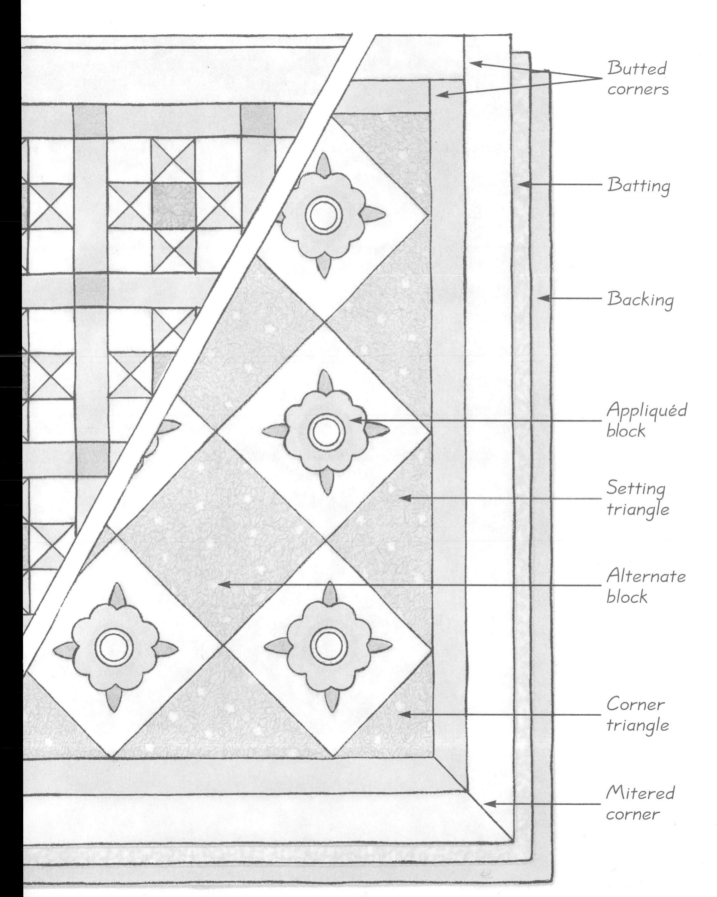

Butted corners

Batting

Backing

Appliquéd block

Setting triangle

Alternate block

Corner triangle

Mitered corner

Rodale's Successful
Quilting Library®

# Creative Guide to Color & Fabric

*Jane Townswick, Editor*

Rodale Press, Inc.
Emmaus, Pennsylvania

## OUR PURPOSE

*"We inspire and enable people to improve
their lives and the world around them."*

Book Producer: Eleanor Levie,
    Craft Services, LLC
Art Director: Lisa J. F. Palmer
Editor: Jane Townswick
Writers: Judith Doenias, Cyndi Hershey,
    Mary Anne Jordan, Linda Lee,
    Diane Rode Schneck, Susan L. Stein,
    Janet Armstrong-Wickell, and
    Darra Duffy Williamson
Photographer: John P. Hamel
Illustrator: Mario Ferro
Copy Editor: Erana Bumbardatore
Indexer: Nan Badgett
Models: Barbara W. Emmett, Jean S. Lefkowitz,
    JoAnn Smith, Nancy Van Ness

*On the cover:* Spring Comes to
    Lee's Market, by Diane Rode Schneck
*On this page:* detail, Night Lights,
    by Deon Marion

**Rodale Press, Inc.**
Editorial Manager, Rodale's Successful
    Quilting Library: Ellen Pahl
Studio Manager: Leslie M. Keefe
Photography Editor: James A. Gallucci
Series Designer: Sue Gettlin
Manufacturing Manager: Mark Krahforst
Manufacturing Coordinator:
    Patrick T. Smith

We're always happy to hear from you.

For questions or comments concerning
the editorial content of this book,
please write to:

    Rodale Press, Inc.
    Book Readers' Service
    33 East Minor Street
    Emmaus, PA 18098

Look for other Rodale books
wherever books are sold. Or call us at
(800) 848-4735.

For more information about Rodale and
the books and magazines we publish,
visit our World Wide Web site at:
    http://www.rodale.com

**Library of Congress Cataloging-in-Publication
Data published the first volume of this series as:**

    Rodale's successful quilting library.
        p.  cm.
    Includes index.
        ISBN 0–87596–760–4 (hc: v. 1:alk paper)
        1. Quilting. 2. Patchwork. I. Soltys, Karen
Costello. II. Rodale Press.
    TT835.R622 1997
    746.46'041—dc21                    96–51316

Creative Guide to Color & Fabric:
    ISBN 1–57954–191–7

Distributed in the book trade
by St. Martin's Press

2  4  6  8  10  9  7  5  3  1  hardcover

# Contents

# Introduction

When I first learned to quilt in the early 1980s, I started out by making traditional patchwork quilts. I love my first quilts, but in terms of color, they were so regulated that they are boring by today's standards. They have been well used, but certainly wouldn't be held up or photographed as examples of stunning color combinations. I faithfully followed the "rules" of color that I knew then, such as not combining red and orange, and not mixing too many shades of green together. I believed, as did many others, that stripes and plaids should never be used together.

I moved on from patchwork and delved into hand piecing, hand quilting, and then hand appliqué. As my quiltmaking evolved, I began to learn more about what I could do with color and fabric in quilts. I finally got past the limitations of those old-fashioned color edicts. My color and fabric sensibilities have changed and grown right along with my areas of expertise. I've never stopped learning or experimenting, and I'll never stop loving color, fabric, and quilting!

As quilters, we are always eager for information that helps us make wonderful quilts. For this book, we asked several of today's top quiltmaking experts, designers, and teachers to share their innovative and creative approaches to color and fabric. Each chapter was a treat for me to read and a source of inspiration. I found myself wanting to head for my fabric stash with scissors in hand to design and stitch a new appliqué block! I have taught quilting classes for many years, and I currently teach about my passion, hand appliqué. This has helped me understand how tricky color can be, both for beginners and for those who are further along in their quiltmaking adventures. We each have a unique set of preferences for color and fabrics, and this book will help you to do more with a favorite palette. You'll also be challenged to try something completely different and out of your comfort zone.

There are several good places to start. If you have a particular space where you want a quilt to go, take "The Decorator's Approach." In this chapter, interior designer Linda Lee shares many of her trade secrets. Anyone who just adores touching and collecting fabrics will enjoy "The Fabric Lover's Approach," by Darra Duffy Williamson. Check out the basics of broadcloth in Cyndi Hershey's chapter, "Schooled in Fabric: Quilting Cottons 101," or take an adventurous route in "Choose the Unusual." The chapter "In the Mood: Color Me Happy!" by Diane Rode Schneck shows how you can let color create many moods in your quilts, from whimsical to romantic, from somber to wild. The chapter "Vary the Value" explains how a wide range of light, medium, and dark colors will highlight and enhance any quilt design and make color schemes more exciting. In "Judging Color: It's All Relative," Judy Doenias takes the study one step further.

To see how to use solid colors and those gorgeous hand-dyed fabrics, turn to Susan Stein's "Significantly Solid" chapter. If you adore prints, you'll be mixing them with confidence after playing with the ideas in "Prints Charming." I particularly enjoyed Janet Wickell's innovative approach to mixing and blending colors by value in "Scrap Quilts with Style." Be careful— it may change the way you make scrap quilts forever!

If you've ever longed for a fabric that just wasn't available in any quilt shop, don't miss Mary Anne Jordan's chapter, "Design Your Own Fabrics." Personally, I can't wait to get my hands on a set of textile paints, some masking tape, and some blue gel glue, to create fabrics for the flowers in my next Baltimore album quilt!

Keep this book handy, and leaf through it whenever you want creative inspiration. You may find that new thoughts and ideas leap off the page and right into your next quilt!

*Jane Townswick*

Jane Townswick
Editor

# 20 Top Tips for Color & Fabric

1 Coming up with color combinations for making quilts to decorate a room can sometimes be slow going. Trust your immediate or gut reactions. What you love initially will only get better with age. Color schemes you don't like won't "grow on you." It's almost always best to scrap them and start over!

2 Try living with a color scheme before you begin cutting pieces for a quilt. When you've chosen a group of fabrics you think you might like together, place the whole grouping where the quilt will be, spread out on the same plane. Glance at your selections every once in a while over the course of a few days. You may decide to make changes, or you may conclude that you've achieved the perfect combination.

3 Use a commercial tan or gray dye to overdye fabrics that seem garish, overly busy, or that have a contrast level that is too high to suit your taste or your project.

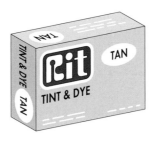

4 Plexiglas value finders, sometimes called ruby beholders, are great for analyzing the relative lightness or darkness of fabrics, and their small size makes them easy to tuck into a tote bag for shopping. Look for them in quilt shops and mail order sources, or visit your local stationery store and purchase clear plastic or acetate report covers in red and green.

5 Look to the great masters of art for help in coordinating colors—imagine a quilt in colors suggested by Monet, van Gogh, or Matisse! Attend art gallery exhibits or browse through books on art, and find a photo of one of your favorite paintings. Match the colors in your next quilt project to the painting you've selected.

6 Running out of a certain fabric isn't always the end of the world—sometimes it can be a blessing in disguise, forcing you to consider other (possibly better) solutions for blocks, sashing strips, borders, or bindings. You can often substitute another fabric of similar color, value, and texture. The difference may be so subtle as to be negligible, but it may also create more visual complexity and interest.

7 Make a series of fabric "flash cards" with large, blank index cards. Glue small swatches of fabrics from your stash to each card. For example, you may wish to keep all the fabrics of the same color on a card. Or combine fabrics by pattern: one card featuring florals and foliage; another with geometrics, stripes, and plaids; a third with nature prints; and so on. Keep these flash cards near your design wall for easy reference when you are choosing or modifying fabrics for a quilt.

8 Avoid the "can't see the forest for the trees" syndrome. If you're nearsighted, take your glasses *off* to judge the overall feeling of the patterns and colors of a fabric, and how they'll look from across the room. If you do not wear glasses, simply squint at fabrics to get the same effect.

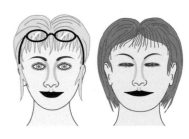

**9** Don't overlook the power of neutrals! Seemingly nondescript whites, creams, beiges, grays, and blacks can coax most colors to blend together easily.

**10** When you are working with a color scheme from only one side of the color wheel, you can all too easily end up with a quilt that lacks interest and excitement. To counterbalance this effect, cross the color wheel and add a color opposite to one of your quilt's colors. Use this color in small amounts, just as an accent.

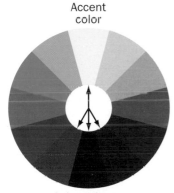

Accent color

Color scheme

**11** Consider incorporating home decorating or fashion fabrics in a wall quilt. Although these fabrics are often heavier than regular quilting cottons, they offer patterns and textures that will make your design unique.

**12** If you find a fabric you really love, buy a yard of it. Purchase quarter-yards of numerous fabrics on a regular basis. Smaller pieces of fabric are great for scrap or appliqué quilts, and one-yard pieces are often enough for the borders on a wall hanging.

**13** Florals with several colors are usually great starting points. Choose one, and build a quilt around it. Simply find fabrics that have one or two colors in common with the floral.

**14** Analyze your stash for gaps in both color and fabric type. Take notes on the kinds of fabrics you own and how much you have of each. Find some quilting friends who are willing to do the same thing, and then get together for an afternoon or evening of fabric swapping.

**15** Mixing patterns is a great way to add interest to a quilt, particularly if it will be displayed in a room with only ordinary architectural features. A foolproof way to start is with a collection of prints from the same company, designed to coordinate. Soon you'll feel comfortable adding other fabrics.

**16** Don't be afraid to include large-scale prints like paisleys, ethnic patterns, pictorials, or other contemporary fabrics in traditional scrap quilts. When cut into small pieces, entire motifs are no longer visible, but their

interesting lines, curves, and colorations remain.

**17** Stripes are timeless and go with absolutely everything. Checks are good fillers when used in the right size. Plaids tend to be informal and tie color schemes together.

**18** Bombarded with catalogs, advertisements, and other visual stimuli, it is easy to get caught up in decorating trends and impractical looks. Sift through the choices in colors and fabrics, and come to terms with what's right for you, your home, and your quilting style.

**19** If you want to make a bed quilt for a newlywed couple, take the bride-to-be with you when you fabric-shop. Ask her to bring samples of things from her home decor to help guide your color and pattern choices. The resulting quilt is practically guaranteed to become their best-loved gift.

**20** Permit yourself to "break the rules" and choose colors and fabrics that just feel right to you. Creating quilts is not a contest—it's a personal adventure meant to bring you pleasure. Don't forget to have fun every step of the way!

# The Decorator's
## *Approach*

**G**ood design principles are universal, whether they apply to selecting colors and
textures for a particular space or to creating a stunning quilt. Many quiltmakers
start with a need—a specific place where they want to display a quilt. This chapter
is filled with interior designer tricks of the trade to help you plan quilts that will
complement any decor.

# Getting Ready

There are many wonderful options for interior decorating today, and they can all come into play when making an exciting quilt. Would a colorful patchwork quilt fill an empty wall in that breakfast nook? Do you want to make a quilt for a newlywed couple's bedroom? Or a baby quilt to coordinate with a nursery? When deciding where you'd like a quilt to be displayed, ask yourself questions like: What kind of decorating style is involved—casual and informal, whimsical, or elegant? If you're making a quilt for your own home, can you characterize your decorating preferences? Make a list of adjectives that come to mind when describing your likes and dislikes. Your answers will tell you what you need to know to make quilts that suit your style perfectly.

## Begin with an Object

If you're starting a quilt design with a blank slate, here's a way to launch a new decor *and* a new quilt. **Select a patterned object you like a lot that contains at least three colors. This can be almost anything—an heirloom bowl, a favorite item of clothing, or even a vacation photo.** Take this object to a paint store and find paint chips that match the colors in it. Then bring your favorite combination of paint chips to the quilt shop, and look for fabrics that include or work well with the colors in your chosen object.

**THE DECORATOR'S APPROACH**

## Keep an Idea File

**Start an interior design notebook or accordion file folder.** Fill it with decorating and quilting magazine pages that appeal to you, plus snapshots of items you own and cherish. Keep leftover floor materials, like shards of ceramic or vinyl tiles, and scraps of wood veneer and carpeting. Gather wallpaper samples, paint chips, and swatches of fabrics from window treatments and upholstered or slipcovered furnishings. Look through this collection on a regular basis to stimulate your creativity.

## Analyze the Room

*Tip*

Repeat architectural motifs in fabric—echo the rectangular shape of a door in a plaid, or the curves of a round window in a circular print.

Take time to look at the room where you want to display a quilt. Observe the lines, shapes, and colors in it. **Is there a high ceiling that elongates the lines of the walls, or a sloping wall that creates a strong diagonal look?** Is the room large, medium, or small? Are there any rounded door or window tops? How many strong colors or textures can you find? The rocky look of a stone fireplace, the rich hues in a wood floor, or any other visual texture you see can also come into play when designing a quilt.

## Blending In

*Tip*

Use fabric patterns as lively design elements to add visual texture to a quilt made in soft colors.

Decide whether you want a quilt that will stand out, or one that will blend into your decor. **An interesting wall color can function as an effective decorating element, indicating that your quilt should be made in colors that do *not* stand out visually.** To keep a quilt from standing out too much, include at least a few fabrics that match some of the visual textures in the room. Or, stay within the same palette, but contrast pattern with solid color walls.

## Attention-Getters

Decide how you want your quilt to function. **If it will be the focal point of a large room, suit the size of the quilt to the size of the room, and choose fabrics with bold contrasts, dark colors, bright colors, or large-scale patterns to create strong emphasis.** A large space requires a large, commanding focal point, while a smaller room needs a smaller focal point (and only *one*). Measure the available space where you want to display a quilt, to determine the quilt's optimal dimensions.

Wood moldings, floors, and doors, stone or tile surfaces, and metal railings all have color—consider echoing these colors in your quilts.

## Light & Neutral, Bright & Bold

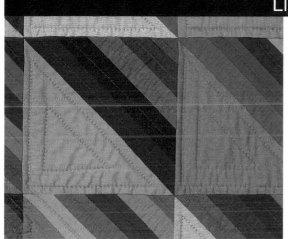

**A good color scheme in interior design usually combines a light, neutral color; a medium, bright color; and a heavy-impact, bold color. The same principle holds true for creating dynamic quilts.** Also, use colors in distinctly different quantities. There should be more of one color than any other, creating a dominant color. Use a second color in a medium quantity and the third color in a small amount.

Preview fabrics in the direction they will be used. Look at bed quilt fabrics horizontally, wall quilt fabrics vertically.

## Consider Lighting

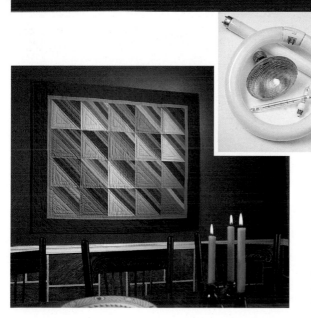

**Look at the prospective fabrics for your quilt in morning, afternoon, and evening light—but especially during the time of day when the room your quilt will be displayed in is most often used. Also, choose light bulbs and fixtures wisely.** Check the color of fluorescent lighting tubes. Deluxe warm white tubes are better than cool white for making colors look natural. Color-corrected light fixtures are widely available, and they're the purest kind of fluorescent light. If you have recessed ceiling lights, consider changing the bulbs to halogen, a crystalline white light that adds life to any color.

Buy quarter-yard pieces of fabrics to take home and test in a room—at different times of day—before committing to purchasing larger quantities.

**THE DECORATOR'S APPROACH**

# The Fabric Lover's *Approach*

I f there is one thing all quiltmakers have in common, it is our love of fabric. We love seeing it, touching it, collecting it…and most of all, using it! So what better way can you think of to plan a great quilt than to choose a fabric you love and make it the focus of a fabulous, one-of-a-kind color scheme? Go ahead! Pull those lush florals, rich paisleys, and exotic batiks off the shelf, and indulge in a fabric lover's dream.

## Getting Ready

The color wheel shown here and throughout this chapter is a good visual tool for understanding relationships between colors and how colors work together. Use it as a helpful guide for choosing successful color combinations of your own. Fabric designers base many of their designs on its familiar color harmonies: the neighbors (analogous colors), the opposites (complements), the triangles (triads), and so forth. Relying on your knowledge of the color wheel, you can select a multicolor fabric and be confident that it will form the basis of a beautiful color scheme.

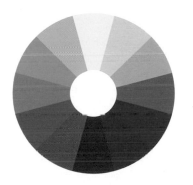

### Possessed

**Make it a habit to regularly take inventory of all of the fabrics you own.** Ask yourself questions like: What colors do I have the most of? The least? Are there any colors missing completely? (You may be surprised!) Does my collection reflect a balance of lights, mediums, and darks in each color? Check for a variety of designs, including florals, foliage, geometrics, dots, paisleys, stripes and plaids, pictorials, ethnic designs, tone-on-tones, and nature prints in a mix of small, medium, and large scales. You'll want patterns that are densely packed, light and airy, randomly printed, and obvious repeat patterns, as well.

## First Love

The key to developing a successful color palette is to start with a multi-color fabric you love—select a special focus print that will act as the core of your color scheme. **An ideal focus fabric is a medium- to large-scale multicolor print, like any of those shown here.** Florals, paisleys, batiks, ikats, border stripes, and tropical or jungle prints all work well. Pictorial, novelty, juvenile, and holiday designs also make good choices.

## Basic Compatibility

*Tip*

Explore the range of prints available to you in "Prints Charming," starting on page 82.

Examine your focus fabric. Which colors make it visually pleasing? How is the balance of color—is there more of one color than another? Take the focus fabric you've chosen to your favorite quilt shop, and look for a variety of supporting fabrics in colors drawn from it. You may want to add only five or six more fabrics, or give yourself the freedom to combine many fabrics to create a scrap look. **In either case, the fabrics you choose should include a healthy mix of light and dark colors, different types of prints, and small-, medium- and large-scale patterns.**

## Endearing Qualities

Don't fall into the trap of over-matching. It really doesn't matter if the pink stripe in one fabric exactly matches the pink rosebud in another, or whether a geometric print contains a brighter green than the leaf in your focus fabric. **Variations like the bright fuchsia, second from the right, offer a pleasant visual surprise when seen at close range, and at a distance, they subtly spark the viewer's interest.**

## The Test of Time

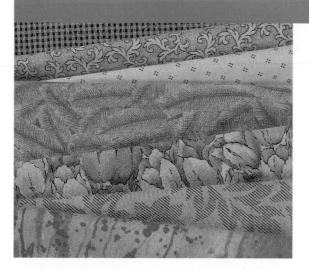

Purchase fat eighths, fat quarters, or other minimal amounts to flesh out the collection of fabrics you already have for a quilt. **Arrange the fabric choices in various combinations around the focus fabric (in this case, the tulip print in the center) to help you decide which one you like best.** Give this decision-making process plenty of time. Let a day or two go by, and then see if you still appreciate how the candidates look together. When you're sure of what you like, purchase larger quantities.

## Dark & Handsome

**Include at least one significantly darker fabric among the accompaniments to your focus fabric.** This will add drama and depth to your quilt. Realize that "dark" is a relative term—if you are working with pastels, navy blue, black, or forest green would not be the best choice for a darker fabric. Just select a richer, deeper shade, such as apple green or teal blue.

## Good Neighbors

You can use a focus fabric and the color wheel *together* to develop a variety of lovely color schemes. **Many focus fabrics, such as the corner squares of this block, feature colors that lie next to each other on the color wheel. Combining these side-by-side colors is a technique that results in a soothing flow of color.** Similarly, focus fabrics and quilts that are based on this kind of color scheme tend to be calming and easy on the eye.

## Sparks of Interest

**Another way to expand your color scheme is to add an accent color.** Also called a sparkler, a zinger, or a complementary color, this is that un-expected fabric—the one that really adds visual "pop" to a quilt. You'll find this color directly opposite one of your side-by-side colors on the color wheel.

## Marriage of Opposites

**Sometimes a focus fabric features two opposite colors on the color wheel.** These color schemes can often be among the most exciting color combi-nations because each color supplies vi-sually what the other lacks. Working with color opposites requires a good sense of balance—the warmer partners (yellow, red, and orange) tend to overpower their cooler counterparts (blue, green, and violet). You'll gener-ally want to use a little less of a warm color so it doesn't domi-nate a design.

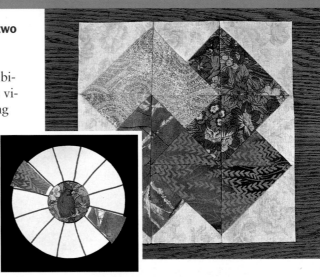

## Different Viewpoints

A focus fabric with a medium- or large-scale pattern will offer many possibilities for cutting patches. Make a window template that reveals the finished patch, and move this template over the surface of the focus fabric. **Take note of any interesting variations. When you find a view that works well for the block pattern you have in mind, simply position the template over that spot in the fabric and mark as many of that shape as you need for your block.** Remember to add seam allowances when cut-ting shapes this way.

# The Quilter's
# Problem Solver

## Agonizing versus Organizing

| Problem | Solution |
|---------|----------|
| You've built a wonderful, diverse fabric stash and don't know how it should be stored to best advantage. | There are many different ways to store fabric. Whichever way you choose, take care to protect your fabrics as much as possible from dust, dampness, acid transfer from wood and paper, and *especially* from sunlight. Here are a few suggestions:<br>❑ Keep fabric in cupboards, closets, trunks, or drawers.<br>❑ Group fabrics by color family.<br>❑ Arrange fabrics according to value (lights, mediums, and darks).<br>❑ Organize your stash by type of print (florals, geometrics, novelty prints, and so on).<br>❑ Separate small scraps from fat quarters, half-yards, and lengths of a yard or longer. |

**Modify a traditional block pattern to make the most of a very large-scale focus fabric.**

Many prints feature large-scale designs. Look for a block pattern that has areas where you can eliminate seams to create spaces big enough to feature oversize motifs. Another option: add diagonal seams to a block to showcase attractive border stripe fabrics. You can often cut unusual fabrics apart and reassemble them to create kaleidoscopic effects, as shown.

## Try This!

**Explore some of these ideas for building a wider collection of fabrics.**

❑ Check garage and estate sales, secondhand shops, and flea markets for fabric and cotton clothing that is in good condition.

❑ Trade fabrics with other quilters by looking through magazine swap columns, browsing the Internet, or suggesting a fabric exchange at your local quilt guild.

❑ Ask traveling family members and friends for fabric souvenirs—and treat yourself to fabric when *you* travel, too!

**B**ecoming better quilters means educating ourselves about more than quilting techniques. Understanding the nature of the fabrics we love best can make all parts of the quiltmaking process easier. This chapter gives you answers to the questions all quilters have, and maybe to some you never thought to ask. Welcome to class!

# Getting Ready

If you are a fabric collector, pull out your stash, and look at it in a different way. For the lessons in this chapter, set aside non-cottons like wool, silk, or rayon. Also separate out any heavyweight cotton fabrics like corduroy, denim, and chintz. The great majority of fabrics quilters use most often are probably broadcloth-weight cottons (regular quilting fabrics). Though similar in many ways, these fabrics may exhibit differences in weave, dye, softness, weight, and quality. Recognizing the unique characteristics of each fabric will help you make the best decisions for your quilts. If you don't have a large stash at this point (but wish you did!), this will help you make wise fabric purchases in the future.

## Fiber Facts

**More quilts are made of cotton fabrics than of any other fiber, because of cotton's many desirable properties.** It costs less to harvest cotton than other natural fibers. It is soft and lightweight, it absorbs moisture easily, and it dries quickly, making it cool in summer and warm in winter. Every inch of a cotton fiber has several hundred twists that help give it a slight stretch and allow for ease in the finished fabric. After it is woven, the base fabric is referred to as greige goods (pronounced "gray" goods).

## 100 Percent Cotton: A+, Synthetic Blends: D-

**Tip**

When testing fabric with matches, keep a bowl of water nearby, for safety's sake.

Quilters love 100 percent cotton fabrics because they're soft and easy to hand- or machine- sew, and they press well. Synthetic blends are fine for clothing but less suitable for quilt-making. Poly-cotton blends increase bearding—the fiber migration of polyester batting that creates a white fuzz on the surface of a quilt. And polyester blends don't hold a crease well, which means you won't get a nice flat appliqué or patchwork seam. **To tell whether a fabric is all cotton or a synthetic blend, hold a lit match to the end of a small piece of it. Burnt cotton leaves an ash that is easily rubbed off, while synthetic fibers will leave a hard, tarlike residue.**

Poly-cotton blend

100% cotton

## Weights & Measures

A high-quality broadcloth (the number one choice for beautiful quilts) generally has a *thread count* of 60 to 68 threads per square inch. Avoid the more coarsely or unevenly woven cottons, which may unravel or lack durability. More finely woven cottons may contain up to 200 threads per square inch. **While their density may make them harder to hand quilt, 200-count cottons produce the best photo-transfer images.**

60-68 threads per inch

40-50 threads per inch

200 threads per inch

## Going with the Grain

**Tip**

Keep the selvages on until you cut your fabrics—otherwise, you'll have a harder time telling the warp from the weft.

Understanding how threads work together in fabric will help you use fabrics to greatest advantage. **Crosswise threads are called the *weft*, while lengthwise threads are called the *warp*.** Each of these directions has unique properties. Across the width of a fabric, there is a slight amount of stretch. Along the lengthwise grain there's very little stretch. **There is almost no stretch along the tightly woven edges, called the *selvages*. The *bias* has the most stretch.**

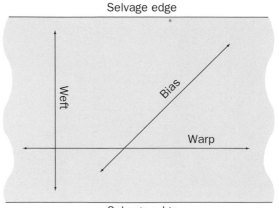

Selvage edge

Weft

Bias

Warp

Selvage edge

## Prints & Dyes

The first step for manufacturers who print fabric is scouring off little hairs on the woven greige goods. Next, fabric is bleached and mercerized, a process that allows the fibers to soften and expand, and also accept dyes more evenly. The quality of the dyes and the number of times fabric passes through the printing process to obtain separate colors affect the cost of the finished fabric. **Fiber-reactive dyes produce the clear, rich, vibrant colors we adore in better quilting cottons. You can expect to pay more for them, but they're worth it!**

## Homespun

A plaid, striped, or checked pattern can either be printed on the surface of the fabric or woven into it. When patterns are printed, manufacturers make every attempt to ensure that the lines of the design align with the grain of the fabric, but this is not always possible. When a pattern is woven into the fabric by using yarn that has been dyed first, the result is a fabric that looks almost identical on both sides, with a pattern that is always on grain. **Homespun is an example of this type of fabric. True to its historical beginnings, homespun colors are usually warm, humble, and earthy.**

*Tip*

See the chapter "Stripes & Plaids," starting on page 76, for more on dyes and directionals.

## Flannels

Even high-quality cotton flannel has a lower thread count than broadcloth. After it is woven, this fabric is run through a napping machine to raise the surface fibers. **This napping process gives flannel its characteristic softness.** Flannels may be single-napped, meaning brushed on one side, or double-napped, with both sides brushed. Before using any flannel fabric in a quilt, make sure to wash it in cool water to shrink and tighten the weave. This will make it more compatible with other quilting cottons.

*Tip*

For a quilt made entirely in flannel fabrics, consider backing it with flannel, eliminating batting and the possibility of bearding.

QUILTING COTTONS 101

## Vintage & Reproduction Prints

The adage "everything old becomes new again" certainly applies to fabric! Both reproduction and vintage fabrics invite a feeling of camaraderie with quilters of the past. **Old *feedsack prints*—from the sacks used to hold flour, sugar, or tobacco from the late 1800s to the 1960s— are still favorites today.** Due to the present ability to produce fabrics with better dyes and finishes, manufacturers are able to duplicate antique fabrics down to the most exacting details. **Reproduction feedsack prints, like those shown in the lower right, look as good or better than their predecessors.**

## Celebrity Designers

Although fabric manufacturers maintain a staff of designers and stylists who generate most of the designs they produce, sometimes other designers create fabric collections. These may be well-known quilters or artists who work very closely with the stylists at a fabric company to have their designs brought to life. **Designers' names are often printed on bolt boards and on the selvages of the fabrics they design.** Some quilters enjoy looking for new fabrics by designers whose work they admire.

## Caring for Cottons

**Tip**

Spray on Quiltgard for UV protection, but keep your best quilts and fabrics away from direct sunlight to prevent the colors from fading.

Wash cotton fabrics to slightly shrink the fibers (an average of 2 percent), and to check for colorfastness. Use *cool* water and a small amount of a gentle, phosphate-free quilt soap, such as Orvus paste. **Hand-wash small pieces of fabric in a sink or basin and lay them flat to dry.** Put larger pieces in the washer on a gentle cycle, and air-dry them to prevent wrinkling. If you do use a dryer, dry fabrics just until slightly damp, and then remove them. Immediately press them smooth with a dry iron.

# The Quilter's
# Problem Solver

## Cures for Creases

| Problem | Solution |
|---|---|
| **After prewashing cotton fabric, it came out of the dryer all creased and streaked.** | The fabric was probably washed with too much agitation and not enough water. Color may also have been ground out along folds. Also, if the fabric twisted in the dryer, the heat may have set creases and faded the dye along the folds. To prevent this, always open up fabric completely before placing it in the washing machine. Be sure there is plenty of cool water in the washer, and set it on a slow or gentle cycle. Do not use commercial detergent, which can leach color from fabric. Dry fabrics on a gentle heat setting, and press them while they're still slightly damp. |

**Get into these good habits to keep your cotton fabrics on the straight and narrow.**

• In general, try to avoid using steam for pressing small patches and blocks. Water can relax the weave of cotton fabric, and the pressure from the iron can stretch and distort shapes.
• Remove selvages before cutting any pieces. Even in seam allowances, selvages can cause fabric to draw up or pucker.
• Cut borders on the lengthwise grain of the fabric whenever possible, so they won't stretch or flare during the finishing process. You'll avoid puckers when adding the binding, too.

## Try This!

**Here's a slick trick that works because cotton's weave allows it to be manipulated easily. Use it when you need to sew together two pieces of fabric and one is slightly larger than the other.**

Start by pinning two patches together precisely at both ends of the seam line. You can disburse any extra fullness by placing several more pins between the first two. With the larger piece on top, spray the fabric lightly with spray sizing. Cover the patches with a clean piece of muslin, and press with an iron until dry. Remove the muslin, and you'll find that most of the extra fullness is gone! This process is called "spot shrinking," and it works like magic!

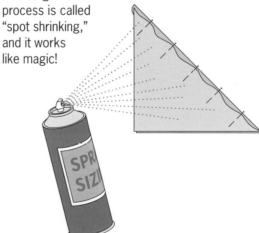

# Choose
## *the Unusual*

Feeling adventurous? Bring your quilting cottons for security, but take time to explore the limitless possibilities in other parts of the fabric universe. 3–2–1...blast-off! Catch a glimpse of the heavenly effects of silk and lamé, the sheer flights of fancy in embellished organdy. Still up ahead: the outermost reaches of velvet, Ultrasuede, and tapestry! Quilters everywhere are discovering how to navigate with nontraditional fabrics for patchwork and appliqué quilts that are out of this world.

# Getting Ready

Start your journey with a visit to a fabric store that carries both fashion and home-decorating fabrics. If you're used to shopping for only quilting cottons, browse through the bridal and formalwear fabrics. You'll find all kinds of fibers, finishes, and textures—from sheer, iridescent, and shiny to matte, metallic, and textural. How about adding a bit of sheen to a quilt with taffeta or sateens? And keep on the lookout for other irresistible finds, like silk, lace, velvet, and even fabrics usually reserved for upholstery or draperies. All of these choices can become something special in a quilt. Don't be afraid to experiment with fabrics you've never used before—exploring the possibilities is what it's all about.

## What You'll Need

**Assorted fabrics of all types and fibers**

**Lightweight, fusible interfacing**

**Iron**

**Press cloths**

**Quilting needles**

## Crazy Quilts

If you're thinking, "I can't use those fabrics in a quilt!" then it's time for a blast from the past. Take a look at some antique crazy quilts, whose creators understood that a wide assortment of fabrics can work together to create a beautiful, complex tapestry of textures. **These Victorian wonders, made strictly for decoration, frequently contained everything from silk, satin, velvet, and brocade to lace, ribbons, and trims.** If you're concerned about mixing many different kinds of fabric together in one quilt, let crazy quilts inspire you!

## Will It Work?

**Tip**

Hand stitchers: Take a few quilting betweens or sharps along when you shop, to see how various fabrics needle.

**When shopping for out-of-the-ordinary fabrics, make up a checklist.** Ask yourself how you will use the fabric—for appliqué or patchwork? Will the fabric require stitching by hand, or can you machine stitch it? Will it need interfacing? Can the fabric be ironed? If not, can you place it somewhere in a quilt where this will not be a problem? It's always a good idea to ask for (or purchase) small amounts of nontraditional fabrics so you can experiment with them at home before committing to larger amounts.

## Test Run on Interfacings

**Tip**

Try using both black and white fusible cotton interfacing. Each creates a different effect, especially with sheer fabrics.

Soft and sheer fabrics like silk, rayon, and tissue lamé open up new worlds for quilters. **To prevent stretching or distortion, stabilize lightweight fabrics by fusing interfacing to their wrong sides.** This will make them as easy to use as cotton broadcloth. Look for lightweight woven or knit fusible interfacings. Test-fuse a small piece, following the instructions supplied by the manufacturer. After fusing the interfacing in place, the fabric should be smooth. If it bubbles or puckers, reduce the heat setting on your iron.

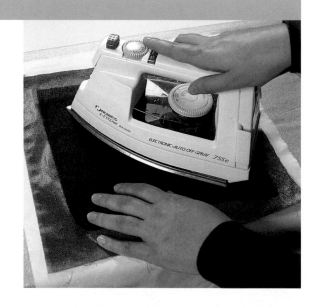

## Lamé & Other Metallics

**Tip**

Stitch metallic fabrics by hand or machine, but don't iron them without using a press cloth— the metals will melt or lose their shine.

Energize your quilts with glints of gold or silver, or metallic red, blue, green, or purple! **Tissue and tricot lamé, as well as other metallic fabrics, lend an opulent glow to patchwork and appliqué quilts.** While it may need interfacing, thin, crisp, woven tissue lamé is easier to work with than tricot lamé, which feels rubbery and is bonded to a stretchy knit backing. Another easy-to-use choice is cotton lamé, an imported fabric woven of both cotton and metallic threads. Because it is 50 percent cotton, it handles well and can be used without interfacing.

## Sheer Fabrics

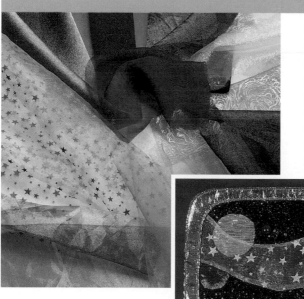

**Tulle, netting, organdy, chiffon, and openwork lace can be transparent, translucent, or ethereal.** These qualities make them work best in combination with other fabrics, rather than by themselves. Be aware of what will show through them. **For example, if you hand appliqué a sheer cloud of organdy on a skyscape, the turned-under seam allowances will be visible and should look neat.** Consider using sheer fabrics as overlays for pieces of opaque fabric.

*Tip*

Stitch blue and green netting over a patchwork seascape. Use lace as ice crystals in a winter appliqué. Try using chiffon to suggest a rolling fog.

## Silks

**Many different kinds of silk are appropriate for quilts.** Silk doupioni, shown at the near left, has a nubby woven texture and a crisp finish; it's available in rich colors. You may find iridescent silks that change color depending on how light strikes them. Occasional nubs and slubs give silk noil an informal elegance, while China silk is soft and fine. In any variety, pure silk is universally unchallenged for absorbing and showing off dyes vividly.

*Tip*

You can handle many firm silk fabrics, like doupioni, taffeta, and some weights of satin, just like regular quilting cottons—no interfacing is needed.

## Napped Fabrics

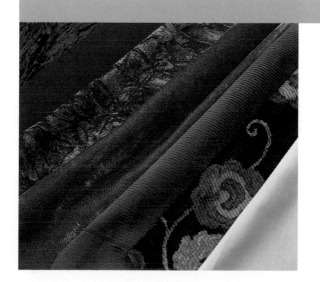

Several fabrics are woven with loops of yarn that are sheared to create a soft, raised surface. **These soft, dense fibers absorb light and add sumptuous depth to a quilt.** Velvets and other napped fabrics can be harder to handle because of their thickness, and they should be steamed, not ironed, to avoid flattening the nap. But their richness makes it worth the effort to include these fabrics in quilts. Crushed velvet and cut velvet are elegant and luxurious. Corduroy, the country cousin, offers soft texture in a casual mode.

*Tip*

Use cotton velveteen, rather than stretch velour, as an inexpensive alternative to velvet.

CHOOSE THE UNUSUAL

## Fancy & Formal

Add shimmer and shine to your quilts with all manner of glitzy, embellished fabrics. **Posh choices include embroidered silks, chiffon embellished with sequins, and organdy with a glittery finish.** In most cases, the foundation fabric is thin enough to be stitched easily by hand or machine. Take caution: Machine sew around, rather than through, sequins; watch out for the stretchiness of knit backings; and never touch the iron directly to these fabrics.

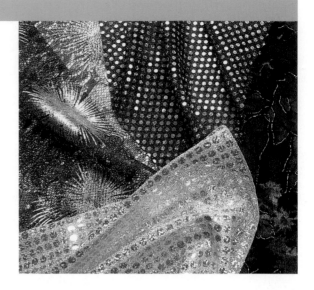

## Wool

*Tip*

Make use of "nostalgia" items: "felt" your child's tattered, old wool sweaters or mittens.

In folk-art quilts, 100 percent wool fabrics have become popular for both appliqué and pieced designs. **Making a project with plain and felted wool can produce a wonderful interplay of textures.** Dry-clean wool to maintain its original appearance. For felt, you can use either a commercial wool-blend, or wool you "*felt*" yourself: machine wash and dry wool, woven *or* knit, using hot temperatures and plenty of agitation. Felting gives wool a tighter and thicker weave, softer feel, and edges that won't ravel when cut.

## Home Decorating Fabrics

**Search for unusual textures, large-scale chintzes, and other prints.** Most home decorating fabrics are much heavier than normal quilting fabrics, so make sure to test them with a quilting needle if you plan to hand-quilt them. Many decorator fabrics are treated with a stain-resistant finish, which gives them a polished-looking sheen. You may want to machine wash home decorating fabrics before using them in a quilt. The finish will usually wash away, but the fabrics may become softer and easier to work with.

## Tapestry Fabrics & Other Riches

**Woven tapestry fabrics may remind you of the elaborate hangings that warmed medieval castle walls.** Along with impressive jacquards and elegant damasks, tapestry fabrics are often used in upholstery, in jackets and vests, or for purses. You'll find many interesting weaves of all kinds of fibers. Hand quilters beware: Tapestry and other unusual home-decorating fabrics are often too stiff or dense to stitch easily. Tying may be a better option.

## Ultrasuede

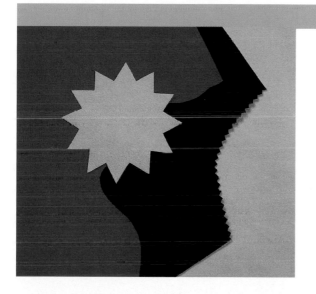

Ultrasuede is a branded, washable material that simulates the softest type of leather. It is great for appliquéing details that might be too small or intricate to stitch in broadcloth. **Because it is not a woven fabric, Ultrasuede will not fray, which means you can cut appliqués to the finished size and stitch even the tiniest shapes without turning under any edges.** This luxurious fabric is available in a wide range of colors. It is expensive, but fabric stores sometimes sell smaller pieces at affordable prices.

## Vinyl

Vinyl comes in solids, tablecloth-prints, and prismatic variations. Because of its rubbery texture, it won't fray, and seam allowances for appliqué are unnecessary. **Pins and stitches will leave permanent holes in vinyl fabrics, so position pieces with a gluestick or masking tape, rather than with pins or basting stitches.** Stitch very carefully by hand *or* by machine to secure pieces in place.

*Tip*

When piecing with thin vinyl or Ultrasuede, finger-press the seam allowances to make them lie flat. Never touch these fabrics with a hot iron.

CHOOSE THE UNUSUAL

# In the Mood:
## *Color Me Happy!*

I
t's impossible not to associate colors with feelings—think of evocative phrases like seeing red...green with envy...in the pink. Paint companies capitalize on associations like these when they give colors names like Sand or Ocean Blue. And when the element of pattern combines with color, your quilt can reflect what you're feeling and put viewers in a certain mood. In this chapter, we'll explore this language of color—and fabric.

# Getting Ready

Color sends subliminal messages about everything—whether it's the color of art, architecture, clothing, home decor, or of products we purchase in stores every day. To start thinking about color in this way, browse through a store where color would normally *not* be your first consideration—like a grocery store, hardware store, bookstore, or pharmacy. Look at the colors you see there. Think about how they attract you, and take notes on your thoughts and observations for future reference. For example, in a grocery store, do you notice that cleaning solutions, shampoos, and toothpastes often come wrapped in cool, refreshing blues and greens? Aren't you likely to see hot, spicy foods packaged in fiery red and yellow? This exercise will show you how color creates moods everywhere we go.

## What You'll Need

**Fabrics in warm and cool colors**

**Large-scale print fabrics**

**Novelty fabrics**

**Juvenile fabrics**

**Regional fabrics**

**Ethnic prints**

## Temperature & Temperament

Take advantage of a color's temperature to send specific messages and create certain moods in your quilts. **The cool side of the color wheel— blues, greens, and purples—can produce calm, restful, and refreshing effects. Think of a mountain forest with a beautiful waterfall, or an island paradise.** Let the warm side of the color spectrum (reds, oranges, and yellows) find their way into your quilts, too—they can express the heat of passion, excitement, or simply the warmth of a sunny disposition.

## Color's Many Meanings

**Consider some of the physical, emotional, and cultural meanings often associated with color, and think about whether you want your quilt to convey some of these things:**

❑ Red: hearts, roses, heat, anger, stop lights, passion

❑ White: light, snow, purity, lace

❑ Orange: autumn leaves, pumpkins, flames, fresh citrus

Think about the concepts each of these colors conjure up for you: Yellow? Green? Blue? Violet? Pink? Brown? Black?

## Living with Color

*Tip*

Look at photos of people standing near the quilts they have made, and note whether their clothing matches colors in the quilts—this is no coincidence!

We all like having the colors we love around us. When our clothing, home decor, and quilts reflect our personal color tastes, we are more comfortable in our surroundings. For a wall quilt or lap quilt that will be used in a high-traffic area, like a living room or den, think about how the colors will play off the room and the people in it. **For a positive impact on your moods, make quilts for your home in a palette of the colors that look best on you and that enhance the natural coloring of your skin tones.**

## Geographical Influences

Where do our color likes and dislikes come from? Personal preferences often originate from places where you live now or where you grew up. And different climates produce different kinds of light, which affect how we perceive all colors. A woodsy, rural area can give you an innate fondness for greens, blues, and natural tones. **If your home is in New Mexico or Arizona, the classic, earthy, Southwestern palette of terra-cotta, gold, clay red, and stone beige probably has a direct influence on the colors you select for your quilts.**

## Souvenir Fabrics

When you travel, visit the local fabric shops! Note the solid colors and the prints, based on the geography, the plant and animal life, plus the tourism highlights of the area. **You may encounter arrays of watery blues, seascapes, and nautical prints at stores in coastal areas. In a rural quilt shop, you'll probably find more florals and nostalgic country scenes, while in New York City, you'll find a greater number of black and gray prints.** The quilts you make with these fabrics will bring back all those wonderful vacation memories.

## Motion & Emotion

Lines and shapes are also important for creating a mood with fabric. **Curved lines and flowing shapes are all restful and soothing to the eye. On the other hand, jagged lines and scribbles that vibrate with life are stimulating.** Compare a sedate, floral print or orderly polka dot with fabrics that feature spiky lines or random, quirky shapes. The eye can rest on neat rows or soft, undulating forms, but angles and squiggles make the eye move, creating a feeling of energy, or even distress. Any and all of these things can make a quilt relaxing or exciting.

It's not necessary to change colors to rev up a quilt that lacks zip. Graphic designs can do the trick.

## Print Size Matters

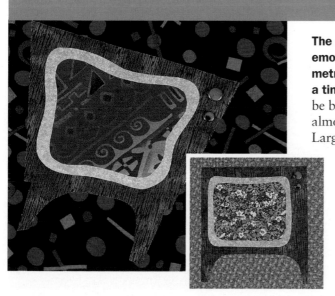

**The scale of a print also affects our emotions. For example, a large geometric is bolder and more graphic than a tiny little print.** Small calicoes tend to be busy, yet without much impact—almost like static on a TV screen. Large designs can add punch and zing.

With pieced quilts, every same-size patch you cut from a large-scale fabric might show off a different part of the print, creating an unpredictable and exciting effect.

IN THE MOOD: COLOR ME HAPPY!

## Aptly Named

Add a personal spark of wit to patchwork by using pictorial prints and theme fabrics chosen to go with the subject or the pattern of your quilt. **How about a Puss in the Corner block using cat prints,** or a Shoo Fly block including bug prints? Maybe Irish Chain blocks with shamrock prints or Road to California blocks with car motifs are just your thing. These little touches are an invitation to look closer and a nice payoff for the viewer. Think of the possibilities based on quilt block names alone!

## Novelty & Juvenile Fabrics

**A step beyond pictorial fabrics, these large-scale prints (which are frequently humorous or designed for children) are a dash of pure fun in a quilt.** Subject matter ranges from food, animals, and sports to hobbies and cartoon characters. Add a piece or two to a scrap quilt, just for the fun of it. Incorporate motifs that call to mind your husband's favorite sport, your daughter's hobby, or the family pet. Even the tiniest little piece will mean something special to the recipient. It's like sharing a private joke or sending a secret message to someone you love!

## Exotic Sophistication

Let people know how worldly you are—or wish to be. Spice up your quilts with fabrics inspired by the Far East, Africa, Europe, or Latin and South America. **Consider rainforest motifs, like tropical foliage and animal prints. Create an air of mystery with faces whose thoughts cannot be known; try dense forest foliage or parasols that conceal what is beneath them.** Take advantage of today's wonderful ethnic prints, African-inspired motifs, batiks from Bali, and graceful Japanese-style pictorials.

36

# The Quilter's
# Problem Solver

## Creating Atmosphere with Quilts

| Problem | Solution |
|---|---|
| **Choosing colors to create a specific mood for a room is difficult. Where should I start?** | Start by analyzing the room where you want to display your quilt. How large is it? What kind of atmosphere do you want to create in the room? If you're looking for a peaceful, quiet refuge, choose a gentle, relaxing palette—soft colors can lighten a dark corner and give an air of meditative calm to a bedroom or den. If you want to create a more invigorating effect, choose warmer, livelier colors. A brightly colored wall quilt hung near a dining room table can animate the room like stimulating conversation. There's no right or wrong way—just let your emotions be your guide. |

**Skill Builder**

**Avoid the rut of making quilts that express the same mood. Challenge yourself to use a type of novelty fabric you've never tried before as the focus of a quilt block.**

If your quilts are usually tranquil and soft, plunge into creating a block that features a silly or funky print. If, on the other hand, you generally prefer a riot of colors and patterns, restrain yourself with a graceful, quiet fabric. In any case, you'll stretch your comfort zone and probably come up with a quilt block you really love!

## Try This!

**Make a wall quilt that expresses a single emotion.**

Joy, peacefulness, anger, passion, sorrow, fear, love—all feelings can be expressed in quilts by way of color and pattern. Try and interpret one of these emotions in cloth. Think first about the colors, motifs, and patterns you associate with that emotion, and then gather together as many fabrics as you can for making a small quilt that represents it. This would make a great challenge for a quilt group or guild.

# Vary the *Value*

Never underestimate the importance of value. Careful and deliberate arrangement of light and dark fabrics is the real secret to the success of any quiltmaking project. This chapter will plant the seeds for lots of ideas that use value to help your color combinations blossom into full flower.

## Getting Ready

The term *value* refers to the lightness or darkness of any color. Surprisingly, it is more often color *values*, rather than the actual colors themselves, that cause a quilt design to emerge visually. Haphazard value placements usually result in a jumble of unrelated shapes. Think about where you want to place light, medium, and dark fabrics in a quilt before you start cutting fabric. After you have determined the pattern you want to make, decided on your basic color scheme, and created a map for placing color values, make up a sample block to test your plan.

- **Various light, medium, and dark prints and solid fabrics in assorted colors**
- **Value finder**
- **Polaroid or regular camera with black-and-white film**
- **Copy machine**
- **Fabric scissors**
- **Transparent tape**
- **White paper**

### High/Low Contrast

**Choose fabrics that are similar in value when you want individual shapes to blend together, or for areas of a quilt that should not command attention.** You can accomplish this even if the fabrics are different colors or prints. **However, contrast in value is essential when you want to define the pattern of almost any patchwork or appliqué design.** For most quilt projects, be sure to include a good mix of lights, mediums, and darks, whether you're working with just one color family or many different hues.

VARY THE VALUE

39

## Positions of Importance

The placement of values can dramatically alter the appearance of a quilt block. Dark shapes are visually powerful, so look to deep colors for pieces you wish to emphasize. Medium values tend to be more passive, and they work well for backgrounds and other areas to which you do *not* want to draw attention. **Contrast counts here, too—for example, a dark star becomes especially prominent against a lighter background.**

## Light Looks Bigger

### Tip

To play with other, similar illusions, turn to "The Look of Dimension" on page 48.

Value can fool the eye and make a shape appear larger or smaller than it actually is. **For example, a light center surrounded by a dark background in a Churn Dash block looks larger than the *same shape* in a dark fabric against a light background.** This optical illusion occurs because lighter colors reflect more light, causing the shape to appear to expand and seem nearer to the viewer. Experiment with this effect in your next quilt.

## Sorting by Value

### Tip

Don't rely on the background color of a fabric to determine its value. Many black or navy fabrics are lightened by motifs printed on them.

**Analyze your fabrics and determine which ones are lights, mediums, and darks by sorting them into three separate piles.** Disregarding color completely, let one pile represent each of these three main values. Since light and very dark values are usually obvious, start with those, and then make a stack of medium-value fabrics with whatever remains.

## Value Is Relative

Sometimes, no matter how long or hard you try, you can't determine whether a fabric is light, medium, or dark. This is because the value of a fabric is relative, depending upon the values of other fabrics you combine it with. **A medium blue–green print may truly be the medium value when placed between a light fabric and a dark navy print. However, that same medium blue–green will serve as a light value when combined with a strong blue print and a deep, midnight blue.**

## The Lineup

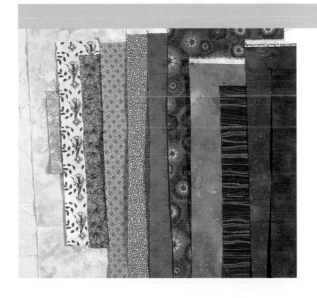

One way to overcome the problem of assigning each fabric a specific value is to determine the *relative value* of all the fabrics to each other. **On a flat work surface, assemble all of the fabrics you've chosen for your quilt, and arrange them in a row from lightest to darkest.** Don't separate colors—it's better if they're all mixed together. Place a blue next to a green or a pink, if necessary—just try to make sure each fabric is progressively darker than the one before it. Continue until your darkest fabric is placed at the very end.

*Tip*

When arranging fabrics by value, stagger the edges by only an inch, making it easier to check for smooth transitions.

## A Magical Tool

**After you've arranged your fabrics according to value by eye, use a value finder to check for accuracy.** This small, transparent, red plastic rectangle will virtually eliminate color, allowing you to focus only on how light or dark each fabric is in relation to its neighbors. You'll find this tool especially useful when value differences are subtle or not visible to the naked eye.

*Tip*

For best results, hold the value finder in front of your eyes, rather than close to the fabric.

VARY THE VALUE

## Right There in Black & White

**If you do not have access to a value finder, another easy way to judge value is to take a black-and-white snapshot of your fabrics. You can also make a black-and-white photocopy of your lineup of fabric swatches on a copy machine.** Either way, the absence of color will enable you to tell at a glance whether you've created a smooth transition in values.

## A Valuable Index

**When you have arranged your fabrics from lightest to darkest, cut a snippet from the corner of each one, and tape the swatches in order of value on a sheet of white paper.** Such a fabric reference sheet will show you the relationship of each fabric to every other fabric in your chosen color scheme. Keep it handy for selecting more fabrics for your quilt.

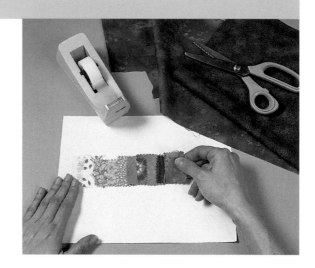

## Just Do It!

**Once you have your fabric reference sheet ready, creating effective color schemes will be easy.** Simply choose one fabric on it to use as a medium value for a quilt block, and pull that fabric from your stash. Select another fabric that appears to the *left* of this fabric, and use that as a light. Finally choose a fabric to the *right* of your chosen medium to function as a dark.

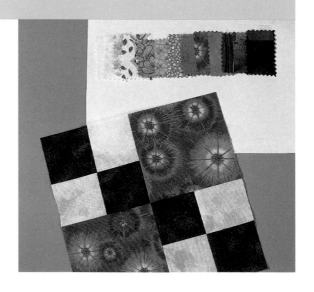

# The Quilter's
# Problem Solver

## Value Judgments

| Problem | Solution |
|---|---|
| **You thought you had the values right, but your finished block no longer looks like the pattern it's supposed to be.** | Try some of these ways to doctor value mistakes and create the look you want in your finished block.<br>❏ Use fabric paint or markers. Brush, dab, or spritz the fabric in certain patches with bleach or dye to make areas look lighter or darker.<br>❏ Alter the value of an area of a block with beads, sequins, or other embellishments.<br>❏ Appliqué a piece of fabric in a more effective value over the offending spot.<br>❏ Quilt (or embroider) heavily with a lighter or darker decorative thread.<br>❏ Experiment with alternate setting ideas. Sometimes the addition of a secondary block or pieced sashing strips and corner squares can revitalize the motif you wanted to emphasize.<br>❏ Think of the oddball block in your quilt as a spark of interest—and add a few *more* of them to keep it company. This is especially effective in a scrap quilt. |

**Skill Builder**

**Make several black-and-white photocopies of quilts you love as they appear in books, magazines, or on postcards.**

Study these photocopies, and ask yourself questions about the values in each quilt: Can you tell at a glance where the dark, medium, and light values are in a quilt, or do the values seem to be mostly mediums that blend together? Does one value seem too prominent, or is there a pleasing mix of all values that makes the design visually effective in black and white? Write down your answers for future reference.

## Try This!

**Design your quilts in black and white.**

If color clouds your ability to judge value, sketch and photocopy multiple line drawings of a quilt block you like. Color in dark values with a black marker, medium values with a gray lead pencil, and leave the light values white. Experiment with different value arrangements, and choose the one you like best. Select fabrics that correspond in value to the black (dark colors), gray (medium colors), and white (light colors) in your drawings.

VARY THE VALUE

# Judging Color:
## *It's All Relative*

C olor is fickle—it can be garish or sedate, bold or quiet—or barely noticeable at all. It's always affected by surrounding colors, by the amount of light that shines on it, and by the color of that light. A color wheel that has 12 basic colors is the simplest way to explain how color behaves. After examining how colors work together, you can take advantage of this knowledge to create the effects you want in your quilts.

# Getting Ready

Refer to "The Fabric Lover's Approach" on page 14 for explanations of basic color terminology and how colors work together. Then take a look at this split color wheel to see how the warm side of the color spectrum is different from the cool side. Warm colors include reds, yellows, and oranges, while cool hues include blues, greens, and violets. Keep these color temperatures in mind when creating color schemes for your quilts. Like many of color's other characteristics, temperature can be relative, influenced by the presence of other colors.

## What You'll Need

**Color wheel**

**Various fabrics in many different colors**

**Plain white paper**

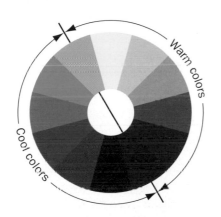

## How Cool Is That!

**A color can appear warmer or cooler, depending on the colors that surround it.** Both groups of fabrics shown here contain the same yellow-green print. In one case, warm colors surround the print and make it appear cooler than the other fabrics. In the other case, the same yellow-green print looks much warmer because it's placed among cool colors, making its yellowness more apparent.

## Optical Illusions

Colors can affect each other in a way that actually changes our perception of the color itself. **For example, look at this small square of medium gray fabric in the center of a larger orange field of color. Then look at another square of the** *same* **medium gray fabric inside a blue area.** Note how the gray squares look like different colors, even though they are actually the same.

## Good Vibrations

Large areas of pure, saturated colors are dramatic. **And when they are placed right next to one another, there is often a feeling of vibration where they meet.** If you want to avoid this kind of dramatic effect, take care not to place large areas of saturated colors right next to each other in a quilt.

The actual juxtaposition

The effect

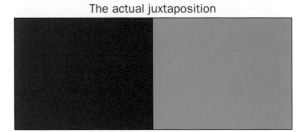

## Afterimages

*Tip*

If the afterimage effect is too great in your quilt design, separate the two neighboring color areas with a strip of black fabric.

As soon as our eyes see a color, they begin to produce an afterimage of it; this is a lighter version of the *complement* of whatever color we're looking at. Test this effect. Working in bright light, draw a black dot on a sheet of plain white paper, and place it over the opposite page. **Stare intently at the tiny black dot in the orange square on the right for 20 seconds. Then move your eyes over to the dot on the sheet of white paper.** You should see a light blue square afterimage projected on the paper. When design wall arrangements produce this kind of blurry afterimage, decide whether the effect is interesting or disconcerting.

## Color Blends

An interesting effect occurs when many small areas of color are placed together. Think of a pointillist painting composed of many dots of color, like those paintings the artist Seurat created. Your eyes naturally blend the points of two very different colors into another color somewhere between the two. And the farther away you stand from the painting, the more apparent the blend will be. **The same effect can occur in fabrics, when small areas of color repeat, as in pointillist prints, very fine stripes, and plaids. In plaid fabrics, a third color appears where the threads of two colors weave past each other.**

## Color Proportions

When you've decided on a dominant color for a quilt, you should select another, secondary color and a third, very different color, for an accent. **Usually, you'll use the largest amount of the dominant color, a smaller amount of a secondary color, and just a bit of an accent color.** Keep in mind that dark, intense, and warm colors tend to be dominant—but you can also make a dull or cool color dominate by using a lot of it. Accent colors are most successful when they provide a high level of contrast to the other colors—use them sparingly for best results.

*Tip*

Liven up a quilt with touches of accent color by liberally using a fabric print that features bits of the dominant color's complement.

## The "Aha!" Factor

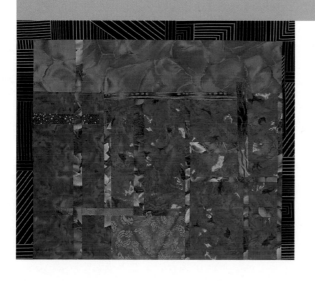

**If you are planning to use a large amount of a particular fabric or color in a quilt, try to incorporate several different fabrics that look similar to it in your design.** Place these "substitutes" in different areas throughout the quilt. At first glance, a viewer will notice overall color—but then the variety of fabrics will become apparent, increasing enjoyment of the subtle variations you have included. This is the "Aha" factor!

JUDGING COLOR: IT'S ALL RELATIVE

# The Look
## *of Dimension*

H ow do our eyes tell us what is near and what is far away? Looking into the horizon will give you the clues for judging distance—and the best landscape quilts exhibit these same effects. Learning to recognize certain characteristics of dimension will enable you to give your quilts, whether pictorial or patchwork, something magical: the illusion of depth.

# Getting Ready

The look of dimension can enhance almost any quilt pattern, from a one-patch pattern to a landscape quilt. Keep the element of distance, or depth, in mind when choosing a pattern for your next quilt project. Seek out patterns that lend themselves readily to a feeling of three-dimensionality, like the Tumbling Block pattern. Consider other shapes, like stars, where you can create a feeling of depth by careful placement of color and value. Or go through your vacation snapshots and choose one as a springboard for a landscape quilt, where you can experiment with the effects of colors and fabrics to create foreground and background areas.

## Graduated in Size

Things that are closest to us appear the largest. As they recede into the distance, their shape remains the same, but their *size* appears to become smaller and smaller. To see this effect easily, look across a vista and see how repeated objects such as trees or houses become smaller and smaller the farther away they are. **You can create this feeling of depth and perspective in a quilt by using graduated sizes of the same shape.**

THE LOOK OF DIMENSION

## Keep It in Perspective

As you are walking or riding down a long road, notice how the road seems to narrow as it continues to the horizon. **To achieve the look of distance, avoid parallel lines.** For landscape, architectural, or scenic quilt designs, choose fabrics carefully for roads, paths, sides of buildings, and other portions that you wish to appear to be stretching back for a long way. Fabrics that are hand-painted or printed in color gradations are useful for conveying the change of light across a distance.

## Gradual Value Changes

Value gradations can increase the illusion of depth in a quilt block. **Note how the use of gradually changing values in these Bull's Eye Square blocks makes them look three-dimensional, and that the direction of this effect changes, depending on where the darkest value begins.** Apply this principle to any shape you want to appear three-dimensional.

## A Matter of Scale

Perspective tells us that the closer we are to an item, the larger it appears. You can add a feeling of depth to your quilts by choosing different scale print fabrics for various parts of your quilt. **Large-scale motifs are best for areas you wish to appear close. Choose medium-size motifs for the middle ground, and small prints for background areas.**

## It's All in the Details

When you look at a tree bough that is close to you, you see each leaf clearly and distinctly, with defined veins and texture, and recognizable shapes. As you get farther away, however, individual characteristics begin to blur and blend, until only the overall impression of foliage remains. Also, things in the distance appear duller and cooler, because the air between you and these far-away objects adds a bluish tint. **To add a feeling of distance to your quilts, use fabrics with sharply defined shapes and patterns and clear colors in areas you wish to appear close. Choose fuzzy, indistinct patterns and shapes, plus duller and cooler colors, for background areas.**

## Overlap

Whenever part of one object is overlapped by another—or at least appears that way—the result is an immediate feeling of distance. In a group of overlapped objects, the one closest to you appears in its entirety. Consider, for example, the quilt block at left. **The three squares appear to be at different distances, with the whole square closest.** Overlaps in patchwork are merely illusions, but you can certainly use real overlaps in appliqué pieces to create the look of depth.

## Make Advances

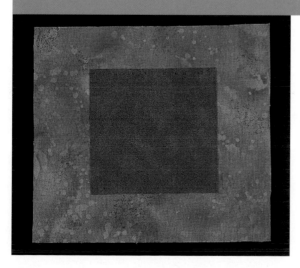

In general, warm colors appear to advance. **Look at the red-orange square (a tone from the warm side of the color wheel) framed with blue-green (a tone from the cool side of the color wheel). Notice how the center square seems to come forward because its color gives it visual prominence.** Use warm and cool colors together to create a sense of dimension.

Refer to the illustration on page 45 for the warm and cool sides of the color wheel.

THE LOOK OF DIMENSION

## Colors in Retreat

**Now look at a same size square inside a frame of red-orange. Notice how the hot-color frame appears to come outward from the cool blue-green center.** This technique could be used to pull the viewer's eye into the center of a medallion quilt.

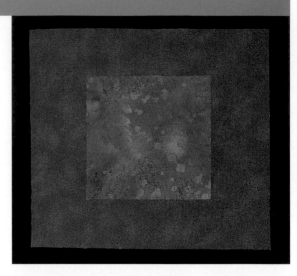

## Reversing the Trend

This warm/cool phenomenon can be switched around by playing with the colors' intensities and values as they relate to each other. **In this example, a blue square, while cool, appears to *advance* even though it is framed by a shade of red, which is a warm color.** The brilliance and clarity of the blue makes it stand out from the toned-down red.

## High Contrast

Both dark and light colors can appear to advance or recede, as long as there is a high degree of contrast between them and their neighboring colors in a quilt. The greater the level of contrast, the greater the sense of depth. **For example, placing a dark emerald green square on a pale green background makes the center appear to advance, due to the high contrast between the colors. However, study the same rich green when it's placed on a blue background that is equally bright. Notice how flat this block looks. When two colors of similar value (even two *different* colors) are placed together, there is little or no illusion of depth.**

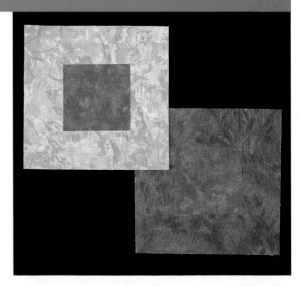

## Shape & Depth

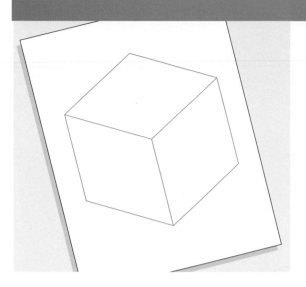

One of the most interesting illusions of depth can be illustrated by looking at the familiar Tumbling Block pattern, where only one shape, a 60-degree diamond, can create a great feeling of three-dimensionality. **Note how the diamonds appear to be three sides of a cube.**

You can buy graph paper marked in squares or diamonds to create Tumbling Blocks and lots of isometric shapes.

## Making Stars or Building Blocks

Although there is only one patch needed to make this pattern, the 60-degree diamond shape proves its versatility when you arrange light, medium, and dark color values in different ways. Play around with patches on a design wall or background fabric. **Use identical or similar values to create a six-pointed star configuration—a wonderful but two-dimensional design. Next, keep the light, medium, and dark values in the same positions for each unit of the Tumbling Blocks design. The results seem amazingly dimensional and complex.**

## Light the Scene

To suggest depth in an appliqué design, consider light and shadow. Determine where to place an imaginary light source…you needn't actually *show* a late afternoon sun or brightly lit lamp. Use subtly striped or striated fabrics to shade surfaces you wish to appear dimensional, placing the darker colors farthest from the light source. Also remember that anything with depth casts a shadow when the light strikes it. **Stitch shadows using black, gray, or lavender sheer fabric.** You could also imply shadows with darker shades of the background fabrics.

For shadow pictures, apply a gray wash of fabric paint where a shadow would fall.

**THE LOOK OF DIMENSION**

# Playing Around
## *on Paper*

**D**rawing and coloring quilt blocks, sashings, and borders on paper *before you cut and sew will let you experiment with lots of colors. At the same time, you can explore innovative approaches to traditional quilt designs and see how colors and patterns interact with each other. Gather up a few easy-to-find design tools, and open your mind to some exciting discoveries!*

# Getting Ready

Before starting to design a quilt, look for inspiration from many different sources. Consider taking some classes at local quilt shops or regional shows. Colleges, adult education programs, art schools, and community centers offer interesting quilt- or art-related courses. Join a quilt group or local quilt guild where you can meet other people who also enjoy designing their own projects. Cut out magazine pages showing quilts you like, as well as other images that appeal to you—such as landscapes or still life scenes. Ideas are everywhere—in tile floors, posters, billboards, clothing, even daydreams. Keep a file of anything and everything that shows design elements you like. Let your mind roam, and transform these images into the basis for a beautiful quilt design of your own.

**What You'll Need**

**Graph paper (4 or 8 squares per inch)**

**Pencils**

**Colored pencils or markers**

**Paper scissors**

**Copy machine**

**Glue stick**

**Straight pins**

**Design wall**

**Construction paper in assorted colors**

**Using a pencil and graph paper, do several line drawings of block patterns you think you might like.** Make each block approximately 2 inches square, so you won't have to color in large areas. Graph paper that has light blue grid lines will usually produce photocopies that show only your drawn lines.

If you're adventurous on the computer, you'll enjoy software programs that help you plan designs, settings, and colors for quilt blocks.

**PLAYING AROUND ON PAPER**

**2**

Cut out your blocks, and experiment with different setting options. **Glue blocks in straight rows on graph paper, allowing space between blocks for sashing strips.** Or position blocks right next to each other. Try setting them on point. Explore the look of alternating plain squares with pieced blocks. You can even use the blocks to create an interesting border around a larger center medallion.

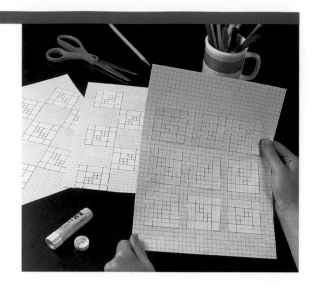

*Tip*

Make color photocopies of a pastel color scheme, then darken some areas with markers. Or play around with a color copier's light to dark settings!

**3**

When you've determined a setting you like, photocopy the page several times. **Use colored pencils or markers to shade various areas in different colors.** Audition some traditional colors, as well as a more contemporary palette. Try out different placements of lights, mediums, and darks. Give yourself permission to create a slightly wild option, or to incorporate an accent color you rarely use. When you've produced several variations, pin them on a design wall and stand back to decide which color combinations appeal to you most.

**4**

When you've determined a color scheme for your blocks, see if you have fabrics in your stash that match it. Use a photocopier to enlarge one of your drawn blocks from Step 3 so that you can make a fabric mock-up of it. Make several copies of the enlarged block. **Cut out the shapes needed for your block in the fabrics you're considering, and glue them onto the enlarged block drawing in various configurations.** Pin these to a design wall to decide which versions you like best. Omit all seam allowances for this cut-and-paste fabric exercise.

## 5

Borders are the frame for a quilt, and deserve just as much creative attention as the center. To play with different border designs, start by counting the number of squares on each side of the quilt setting you chose previously. **On another sheet of graph paper, draw a rectangle with sides that correspond to the size of your quilt design, to represent the inner edges of a border. Draw a second rectangle outside the first, to represent the outer edges of a border.** Make several photocopies of this border pattern.

## 6

To consider color candidates for plain borders, draw some borders on construction paper, and cut them out. **Position these "window frames" over your colored-in quilt setting, to see which border colors you like.** You can also audition construction paper borders in varying widths.

**Tip**

Try extending the lines of blocks into a border, or breaking up a border with strips of fabric used in the quilt center.

## 7

Appliqué quilts can benefit from preliminary paper play, too. **Draw an appliqué design you like on graph paper, make several photocopies of it, and use colored pencils to try out various color schemes.**

**Tip**

To quickly consider non-white appliqué backgrounds, make color photocopies of a design using pastel paper in pink, light green, baby blue, or lavender.

**PLAYING AROUND ON PAPER**

# Making It Up
## *As You Go*

I f you'd like to take your quiltmaking in a whole new direction, start making choices of
your own. This chapter helps you select all the ingredients for a great quilt: color, value,
settings, and more. Even when you do follow a "quilt recipe" in a publication, you'll be
able to play around with design elements and enjoy fruitful results—a quilt that is uniquely
your own.

## Getting Ready

### What You'll Need

**Quilt books, magazines, and photos of quilts for inspiration**

**Assorted fabrics**

**Design wall**

**Straight pins**

**Reducing lens, Polaroid camera, or binoculars**

**Rotary-cutting supplies**

**Fine, felt-tip permanent marking pen**

**Sheets of clear, heavy plastic or acetate**

Before setting out on your own to make an original quilt, there are some tools you should have to make the journey easier. A way of storing fabric so that you can see it at a glance is one way to keep inspirational ideas around you at all times. Another important tool is a design wall that suits your needs. If the space you have available is small, you can make a great portable design wall simply by pinning or taping a piece of flannel onto a door, or by gluing felt over a bulletin board. If you have more room, consider creating a more permanent design wall that can be left out while you do other things. Cover a large sheet of pegboard, foam-core board, or other insulation material with flannel or batting. You might also staple flannel or felt over a simple wood frame or artist's stretcher bars.

## Starting with a Pattern

**1**

**Choose a quilt design you would like to make from a book, magazine, or pattern, and think about how many fabrics you wish to use.** Decide whether the project will go in a specific place or if you just want to make it to play with color. Determine whether you want your quilt to have a planned color scheme or more of a scrappy look.

MAKING IT UP AS YOU GO

59

**2**

**Pull out all of the fabrics from your stash that you think might work for your project**. Include solids, hand-dyes, plaids, prints—even fabrics that may seem a little wild or have only a slight relationship to the other fabrics. You may be surprised by your reactions to the combinations you've created. Think some more about the look you want to create in your quilt in light of the fabrics you already have on hand.

Glue a piece of each fabric you're considering for a project to an index card, and take the card along when you shop for more fabrics.

## Starting with the Fabric

**1**

To plan a quilt by starting with a fabric you have in your collection, **place several other fabrics that might be compatible around it.** Then think about whether these fabrics suggest certain types of quilt patterns. Did you choose prints with a garden theme that might be appropriate for an appliqué design? Does the sheer number of fabrics you've chosen point to a scrap quilt in a geometric pattern? Did you choose lots of related fabrics in both light and dark values that could best be showcased in a sampler quilt?

**2**

Place or pin some fabrics on a design wall. **Take away any that do not please you, and add others until you find a combination that you like.** Leave the fabrics out, and look at them another day, when your mind is refreshed. Compare your first and second responses. Do you still like the choices you've made?

**3**

**To see how your fabrics will appear from a distance, look through a quilter's reducing glass, a Polaroid camera, or the large end of a pair of binoculars.** This will tell you immediately whether any particular fabric will "jump out" at the viewer. It's also a great way to find out whether your fabrics are blending together too much. A mix of light, medium, and dark fabrics will give a quilt interest.

## Playing with Blocks

**1**

If you're thinking about making a repeat-block patchwork quilt, cut out enough patches for one block. Place the patches on your design wall and evaluate your fabric choices. If one fabric stands out too much, try it in another position, or eliminate it. **If you think a color or print is too bold, substitute a quieter one.** Playing with the positioning of fabrics in a block *before* you start to sew can make you much happier with the look of your finished quilt.

**2**

**If you've decided on a scrap quilt that will have a lot of different fabrics in it, make up two or three blocks, and place them on your design wall.** This will help you make sure that you like your fabric combinations and color placements. It can also aid in determining whether to include more of a certain fabric and more or fewer colors. It will also reveal whether an interesting secondary pattern emerges from the combination of blocks.

**Tip**

Red and yellow are real attention-grabbers; use them sparingly in a scrap quilt.

**3**

**If you've chosen an appliqué project, cut out some appliqué shapes, and compare how they look on various background fabrics.** You don't need to cut the background fabrics into blocks—but you might fold them approximately to block size. Look at your choices on your design wall to see if you prefer a higher or lower contrast between the background and appliqués.

*Tip*

Plan to fuse your appliqués? Steam-A-Seam 2 enables you to reposition the appliqué shapes until you're ready to commit to permanent placement.

## Setting the Scene

**1**

After all of your blocks are completed, place them on your design wall and experiment with sashing strip and setting ideas. Try the blocks next to each other, straight or on-point. **Try putting sashing strips and corner squares between blocks.** Alternate pieced or appliquéd blocks with plain blocks cut from solids or prints. Keep experimenting until you come up with a setting you like.

*Tip*

Sashing strips in the same fabric as the background of the blocks will make the blocks appear to "float" on the surface of a quilt.

**2**

If you have decided on sashing strips, explore the effects of pieced or appliquéd sashing. **Try strip-pieced value gradations to create a sashing treatment that will carry the viewer's eye around the quilt.** Flying Geese units and half-square triangles are also popular as sashing strips, and they can set off block designs beautifully.

*Tip*

Curved vines and leaves add a flowing element to sashing strips around floral appliqué blocks.

**When you've decided on a setting, audition some border options.** A wide, plain border is the perfect spot for showcasing beautiful hand quilting. Borders pieced from several colors of fabric can create an effective frame for the center and create a feeling of continuity throughout the quilt. Take note of any fabrics in a pieced border that stand out too much, and eliminate these fabrics.

**Tip**

If your quilt will be used on a bed, the border design will probably fall on the over-hang areas—make them memorable!

## Finishing Touches

**1**

Audition several quilting designs before you decide on any. **Use a design overlay to analyze each possibility, as follows:** When your quilt top is finished, place pieces of clear, heavy plastic over a portion of it, and draw a quilting design, using a permanent, fine, felt-tip marker. Repeat this process with other quilting designs. Some quilts need only functional quilting, while others look great with overall quilting designs. Many quilt tops offer great places for beautiful hand quilting to decorate plain areas or enhance appliquéd motifs.

**Tip**

Quilting thread is available in lots of colors, so consider a nontraditional color and use a pen color that corresponds, on clear plastic.

**2**

**When you are ready to finish and bind a quilt, use a rotary ruler to measure and make sure that the sides and corners are truly square.** Trim the corners or sides if necessary. If your quilt has wavy or flaring edges, add basting stitches to draw up the offending areas to prepare for binding.

MAKING IT UP AS YOU GO

**3**

Cut several strips of potential binding fabrics, and hang them on your design wall next to your quilt. **Consider which ones complete the quilt attractively.** With each candidate next to the quilt, stand back to get a different perspective.

**4**

After binding your quilt, place it on your design wall one more time, to make sure it hangs straight and flat. **If an uneven edge needs a bit of persuasion, mist the surface of the quilt with cold water** and let it dry, or use a steamer to coax it into lying smooth. Leave the quilt on the design wall until it is completely dry.

*Tip*

Use a regular, 35-mm camera to produce a long-lasting record of all your quilts. Such records are good for insurance purposes, as well as for remembrance.

**5**

**Take a Polaroid snapshot of your finished quilt.** Use a copier to produce several images of the quilt. Assemble these to consider a larger quilt, in a whole new configuration. In this way, you could start to make up a brand new quilt.

# The Quilter's Problem Solver

## Storage & Design Wall Solutions

| Problem | Solution |
|---------|----------|
| **You can't keep your fabrics in a place where they can be seen at a glance, so you need a way to keep track of what you have.** | Cut a 2-inch square from each fabric you buy, and glue or tape the squares onto notebook pages. Organize the fabrics on each page by color family, and keep the pages together in a three-ring binder. Note the yardage amount for each fabric you own, and indicate when you have used some. Remember to remove the swatch from the notebook after you've used up the fabric. |
| **You have very little available space, even for a fold-up design wall.** | The flannel backing of a picnic tablecloth or a crib-size piece of batting will make a great design wall. Just pin one of these onto your drapes or tape one to a door, and take it down whenever you're finished using it. This type of design wall has one especially great advantage—you can take it with you to quilt classes and workshops. |

## Skill Builder

**Perhaps some people are born with an innate talent for using color. But others of us can acquire it—with knowledge and experience.**

Learning the "rules" of color does not always translate into a successful quilt. You may need to practice! Why not make small quilts for babies in crisis? Or lap quilts for a veterans' hospital? Select easy, pieced patterns, and experiment with new color schemes while you work. In time, your color sense will develop.

## Try This!

**Make two small quilt tops, identical in everything *except* fabrics.**

Put together two different color palettes. For example, make one quilt top in pastel prints and one in jewel-tone solids. Continue making quilt tops as long as you can come up with new and intriguing fabric combinations. Use the results as gifts. In this way, you'll share what you've learned about color and fabric!

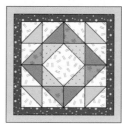 

# Going Solo:
## *Single-Color Quilts*

**Q**uilts in shades of just one color can still have plenty of force. Steer yourself toward any hue that makes your heart beat faster—the mysterious blues of the night sky, the perky yellow-golds of roadside wildflowers, or the tranquil browns of a forest floor. No matter which color you decide to work with, a single-color quilt can be as elegant and exciting as a multicolor rendition. So choose your favorite color, and drive on ahead.

# Getting Ready

Tints and shades of one color, otherwise known as a monochromatic palette, need never be monotonous. Deciding on the mood you want to create in a quilt can help you choose the color you want to feature. Do you want a subdued, restful-looking quilt in cool blue-greens? Or a racy look, in rich reds? You may have enough fabrics in one color in your collection already, since we all tend to buy more of our favorite colors when we shop. If you don't have a large fabric collection yet, visit a paint store and look through color chips. You'll find that paint samples printed in light-to-dark ranges on long strips of paper *are* monochromatic groupings, and you can get a feel for the colors that appeal to you or fit your decorating needs by browsing through them. Whichever color you decide to use for your quilt, choose fabrics in a wide variety of print types, in a range of values and scales.

## What You'll Need

**Range of very light to very dark fabrics in one color**

**Quilt block pattern**

## Select Your Color

**Lay out every fabric you own in the color you've chosen for your quilt.** You may decide not to use all of them, but it's easier to make selections when all the possibilities are in front of you. Go with your instincts—select any fabric you think falls into your color category, even if the different fabrics don't appear to be "good" matches.

## Values Are Vital

**Tip**

Place white or pale tints next to very dark patches. The strong contrast visually pulls the darker elements of the design to the forefront.

**Now line up the fabrics you've chosen according to their color values.** Variations in value are essential for making a successful one-color quilt. Study the arrangement, and think about how you want value to work in your design. You may prefer a subtle variation in value from patch to patch. **However, clear differences in value usually make a quilt block more appealing.** If working with color value is a new experience for you, see "Vary the Value" on page 38 for more detailed information.

## Grayed Shade

**Consider including some fabrics that are grayed versions of the color you've chosen for your quilt.** Often, these less intense colors will take a back seat visually, allowing brighter or more pure colors to drive the design.

## Staying in One Gear

**Tip**

Consider using very narrow, high-contrast sashing strips to unify a monochromatic quilt.

Fabrics for a single-color quilt can be very similar. For example, you might decide to use only linear, directional fabrics, such as stripes and plaids, or geometrics. However, to supply contrast and interest, it's important that these fabrics differ in some way. **Vary the value, including a range of pastel tints to very dark shades for visual high-gear effects.**

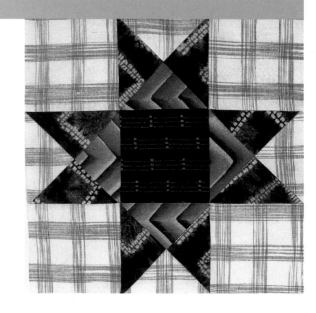

## Scale Up & Down

**A mix of print scales can be the vehicle that carries a single-color quilt.** Large, medium, and small motifs provide interesting variations in visual texture. Where you place small, graphic prints, dominant motifs, and overall design is important. Repetition will generate unity and rev up an old, familiar quilt pattern.

## In Neutral

Adding neutral fabrics to a one-color quilt is one way to increase design options without introducing a second color. Blacks, grays, and whites can contribute a coolness or a contemporary crispness. **Beige will warm up a monochromatic quilt design or give it a sense of age and nostalgia.**

Place darker versions of a neutral color next to bright or bold colors to help soften them in a quilt design.

## Hint at Another Color

Adding just the mere *touch* of another color to a monochromatic quilt can accelerate the excitement without undermining or overpowering the single-color theme. **Try a very dark shade of another color to add a spark of surprise to a monochromatic quilt.**

# Significantly *Solid*

Whether vibrant or subtle, solid fabrics can produce beautiful effects in a quilt—a sense of drama or the illusion of a soft glow. By allowing a patchwork or appliqué design to capture all the attention, solids can make a traditional pattern look cleanly contemporary. And solid fabrics set off quilting stitches and patterns like no printed fabric can. Let's take a tour through some gorgeous solid and "almost" solid fabrics, and discover their potential for adding flair and excitement to your quilts.

## Getting Ready

Go through your stash, and gather together all of the solid fabrics you already own. Mix and match them, and take some time to think about whether you want to throw in some prints as a way to "stretch" the amount of solids you have available for a particular project. If you find gaps in your collection, make an effort to flesh out your color range. Think about collecting not only colors you love, but also shades that challenge you. You'll soon be on the way to loving solids!

**Solid-color fabrics**

**Mottled or "sueded" fabrics**

**Substitute solids: tone-on-tone fabrics that "read" as solids**

**Hand-dyed solids**

**Block designs**

## Off to a Solid Start

### Fill in the Gaps

Surprisingly, solid fabrics can be a bit harder to find than prints—many quilt shops do not carry a large variety. Check fabric shelves often, because solid colors vary from year to year. At quilt shows, look for fat quarters of solids bundled in value gradations. **Start a collection of solids in your favorite colors and make a habit of adding to them on a regular basis.** Also, keep on the lookout for fabrics that are "mostly solid." Whether hand-dyed or commercial, these mottled fabrics have a lot of visual texture.

## Solids in a Starring Role

**Tip**

Piece solids together in a progression of hues to make an interesting border.

Start with a favorite multicolor print as the basis for a quilt, and pick out solid hues that are contained in the print. **When a print fabric is used consistently throughout a quilt, it acts as an effective background for many different solid colors.** Experiment with various arrangements of the solid colors before you zero in on your final choices.

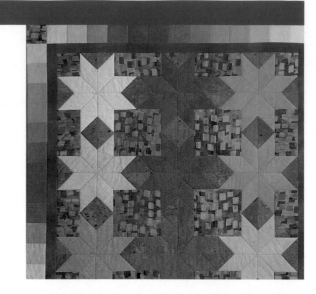

## Solids in a Supporting Role

Solid fabrics can help keep a quilt from looking too busy. **Use a solid as the background of an appliqué block. A strong contrast or a quiet color will showcase the appliqué shapes beautifully.** If the prints are busy, solids will provide welcome resting places for the eye.

## Sampler Blocks

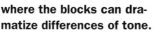

**Tip**

Read "Vary the Value" on page 38 to discover more ways to play with light and dark values of one color.

Shades of one color are easy to mix and match. Packaged bundles in various light, medium, and dark versions, or values, of one color often contain six or eight fabrics, making it easy to plan a block design around subtle contrasts. **Use a range of color values in a sampler quilt, where the blocks can dramatize differences of tone.**

## Go from Dark to Light

Pieced arrangements that shade progressively from dark to light—or vice versa—give a pattern a sense of movement, drawing the viewer's eye from one side to another. **To showcase gradations of color value in graceful ways, choose Fans, Dresden Plates, or Double Wedding Ring patterns.**

Spread solid gradations from the center of a quilt outward—or across the surface—to bring the viewer's eye from one area to another.

## Change Directions

**To create even more excitement, contrast the _directions_ in which you place solid-color gradations in a quilt.** In this quilt, teal shades go from dark to light, while the purples and grays progress from light to dark in the opposite direction. The effect is positively luminous.

## Visit Amish Colors

Because Amish quilts are almost always made in solid colors, geometric patchwork and large amounts of beautiful hand quilting provide the pattern, texture, and embellishment. **To create the look of an Amish quilt, choose jewel tones and saturated hues. Use deep, dark colors like black, dark green, or navy for background areas and narrow borders.**

Count on an Amish-style quilt to bring simple elegance and strength to a home or office.

S I G N I F I C A N T L Y   S O L I D

# A Step Beyond Solid

## Tone-on-Tone Fabrics

Tone-on-tone prints are even more versatile: Flip them over and use the reverse side as a solid fabric.

**Lots of prints "read" as solids when you see them from a distance. For this reason, these fabrics make great "solid substitutes."** If you stand back from small, tone-on-tone prints, none of the fine design lines are visible—you see only the background colors. Use these prints just as you would a plain, solid fabric of the same background color. This is a great way to expand the number of "solids" you have to work with in a quilt.

## Variegated Solids

Check out Skydyes, beautiful hand-painted fabrics by Mickey Lawler. For ordering information, see "Resources" on page 126.

**Consider multishaded and hand-painted fabrics.** Some shops carry the work of a local hand-painter, which can provide you with fabrics that will make your quilts totally unique. Major fabric companies also import these special fabrics. While a hand-painted fabric may contain all the colors of the rainbow, careful positioning of templates will provide lots of different "mostly solid" patches.

## Partners for Solids

Commercial solids that contain no mottling may call for lots of quilting or embellishment.

**Large, unpieced areas in a quilt design are perfect places to use gorgeous variegated or multishaded fabrics, especially if the fabric has several colors in it.** Let various shades fall randomly, or create a planned color arrangement in your blocks. Besides adding warmth and liveliness, multishaded fabrics coordinate splendidly with solid fabrics.

SIGNIFICANTLY SOLID

# The Quilter's
# Problem Solver

## Solids to the Rescue

| Problem | Solution |
|---|---|
| **Your quilt guild wants to make a raffle quilt that will appeal to both men and women, combine traditional style with contemporary colors, and fit into any decorating scheme.** | When the goal is to appeal to the widest audience possible, choose solid colors in a variety of hues and a popular geometric pattern, like Log Cabin or Eight-Pointed Star. Both designs are familiar to most people. Their lines are clean and uncluttered-looking, yet complex enough to allow for lots of creative color combinations. |

**Expand your color awareness: Buy a package of Pantone color sample papers (from an art supply store) and take them apart. Then assign yourself some of the exercises below. The papers will represent solid-color fabrics, and your eye will not be distracted by lines and shapes in prints.**

❏ Pick out some colors you think represent certain moods or emotions, seasons, a garden, a piece of music, a fruit cocktail, and so on.

❏ Think about which colors seem to vibrate visually when placed next to each other.

❏ Analyze how colors look on black, as opposed to white, backgrounds.

## Try This!

**Take one block design and place a solid color in different areas to emphasize different portions of the design.**

You can create many different looks for the same block, simply by changing the position of a single solid color. Cut out enough patches so that you will have plenty for experimentation. Back each piece with fusible adhesive, and iron every combination you create onto a foundation fabric so you can keep them for comparison.

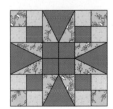

# Stripes
## & Plaids

R emember those conservative, pin-striped shirting fabrics, or that gingham apron your mother wore? If you haven't shopped for striped and plaid cottons recently, you may be surprised at their diversity. While the popularity of humble, country versions has flourished, contemporary dazzlers are also plentiful. Quiltmakers of every stripe are heading straight for directional fabrics!

## Getting Ready

Begin collecting interesting plaids and stripes in colors that appeal to you. Striped fabrics contain parallel lines that go more or less in one direction, while plaids are a network of lines that cross each other, usually at right angles. Both types of fabrics are available in every scale, from dainty to bold, and in patterns that range from calm to busy. They may consist of only two colors, or they may contain a wide array of hues. Since plaids and stripes are popular with almost all quilters, you'll find it easy to gather a considerable assortment at your local quilt shop or from mail order sources. Try to include a variety of scales and color values, and shop for new releases from fabric companies often!

### What You'll Need

**Assortment of striped fabrics**

**Assortment of plaid fabrics**

**Miscellaneous fabrics, in a variety of print types and scales**

## Woven versus Printed

Woven stripes and plaids contain different-colored threads passing over and under each other to form the fabric. These fabrics are reversible; they look the same on both sides. You can also cut out a patch and turn the fabric over to produce a mirror image of the same patch. Printed stripes and plaids are made by applying one or more passes of dye onto the surface of a fabric that is already woven. **It's usually easy to tell whether a fabric is printed or woven: Printed plaids and stripes appear lighter and less distinct on their reverse sides, since the dyes were applied only to their front surfaces.**

You can sometimes correct a misaligned woven stripe or plaid by washing the fabric to relax the fibers and then pressing it, pulling the grain to straighten it.

**STRIPES & PLAIDS**

## Cutting Considerations

Often, a striped fabric needs to be cut carefully so that the stripes flow in the same direction across a pieced block, border, or other area. For example, you can usually cut squares in half diagonally to make half-square triangles that match. **However, many designs, such as the Flying Geese pattern, require half the triangle patches to be cut along one diagonal, and the other half to be cut along the *other* diagonal.** Otherwise, the background areas will appear broken up and disjointed.

## Even & Uneven Stripes

**Striped fabrics can take on many different looks.** The most basic examples feature even repeats of lines that are the same width. These types of stripes often come in two colors, but you can also find multicolor simple stripes. More complex striped fabrics consist of lines in uneven widths. When you look for striped fabrics, consider how you plan to use them in a quilt. Simple, even stripes produce a calming effect, while multi-width stripes create more visual excitement.

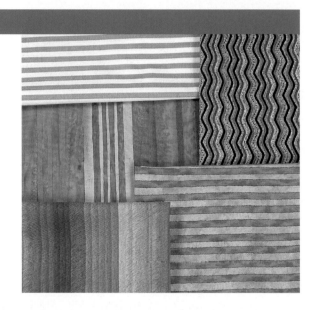

## Diagonals & Curves

Some stripes and plaids are printed diagonally, and some are curved. Such variations completely eliminate the problem of lines that are not precisely on grain. **Diagonal or curved stripes and plaids lend movement and add a touch of life to what might otherwise be rather ordinary-looking block patterns.** Use these types of fabrics sparingly, however, because too many diagonal or curved lines in a quilt can be overpowering.

## Symmetrical & Asymmetrical Plaids

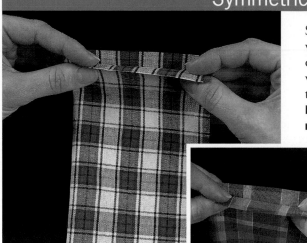

Symmetry is an element to look for when choosing plaid fabrics for an orderly, well-balanced quilt. To see whether a plaid is symmetrical, fold the fabric in half along the grain. **If the pattern in the upper half matches the pattern in the lower half, you'll know that the plaid is symmetrical. If the patterns don't match, it's an asymmetrical plaid.**

Use both symmetrical and asymmetrical plaids in a quilt to create a more interesting visual mix.

## Ikat Weaves

In India, Japan, and South America, master artisans produce skillfully arranged designs known as ikats. Before weaving an ikat fabric, segments of some threads are dyed different colors to create a variegated thread. **For stripes and plaids, the color variations along the length of the threads break up what we usually see as straight lines, creating an interesting, irregular appearance in the finished fabric.** Sometimes threads are dyed a number of different colors, adding even more complexity to an ikat pattern.

In a quilt, ikat fabrics add an exotic flavor, yet blend nicely with domestic stripes and plaids.

## Stripes & Plaids with Other Fabrics

We sometimes have the idea that plaids and stripes do not mix well with other types of fabrics. While it is true that you can make a beautiful quilt using *only* stripes and plaids, don't hesitate to combine them with other fabric types! **Geometrics, florals, and paisleys all work beautifully with directional fabrics.** Mix them together as you would any other fabric types.

S T R I P E S   &   P L A I D S

## Stripes & Plaids as Backgrounds

**Light-colored stripes and plaids are good substitutes for muslin and other traditional background fabrics.** They add visual texture to a quilt, yet they are subtle enough to recede visually and allow other fabrics to dominate. To keep them from calling undue attention to themselves, take a little extra time to match the stripes and plaids, or to center them on the patch.

## Appliqués with Built-In Details

Incorporate the lines of stripes and plaids into your appliqué designs. **Cut patches from directional fabrics purposely, using the lines to represent the veins of leaves, surface ridges of acorn caps,** bark in tree trunks, or striations in flower petals.

## Stripes as "Cheater Cloth"

**In miniature quilts, use striped fabrics to substitute for areas of thin, pieced strips.** You might, for example, cut a half-square triangle from striped fabric for a Roman Stripes block, or cut bars of horizontal stripes for a Chinese Coins quilt. Quilt between the stripes so fabrics *look* as if they are pieced and stitched "in the ditch."

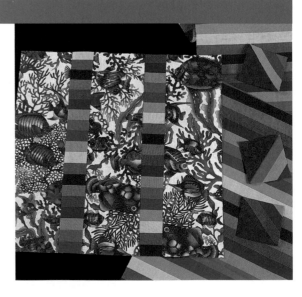

## Calm or Busy

Both striped and plaid fabrics add visual movement to a quilt. The *amount* of movement increases as these fabrics become more complex. Varied line widths, many colors, and the way patches are cut and positioned in a block all contribute to how calm or busy a block appears. **For a calm, structured look, cut pieces so that the lines of a plaid or stripe are parallel or perpendicular to the edges of your patches. For a more whimsical and animated appearance, cut plaid or striped patches with their lines skewed.**

Before joining patches that are cut off-grain, stay stitch carefully along the bias edges to keep them from stretching.

## Directionals for Sets

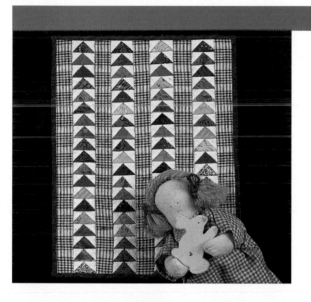

**Use plaid or striped sashing strips to help tie a design together and create a unified look throughout a quilt.** Use stripes to visually shorten or lengthen sashing or lattice strips. Use plaids to bring excitement and complexity to a quilt as a whole.

## Directionals for Finishes

Try some of these techniques to enhance a quilt top with directional fabrics. Cut across chunky stripes to simulate a pieced border. Use even stripes, running lengthwise, to create perfect mitered borders. Make a double border by combining a large-scale plaid or striped fabric with a smaller-scale version. **Stripes and plaids also make wonderful choices for bias bindings.** Turning stripes or plaids on the diagonal provides a zippy edge and complements traditional, folk art, and bold quilt designs alike.

**S T R I P E S  &  P L A I D S**

# Prints *Charming*

L ook around any quilt shop, and you will realize that printed fabrics reign supreme. The wide array of colors and patterns is astounding. As long as you are somewhat sensitive to what makes for a successful mix of color and texture, you can put lots of prints together. Such combinations will make your quilts fit for a king (-size bed), or well-suited to warm the walls of your castle.

## Getting Ready

It's easy to recognize differences between the textures in corduroy, satin, denim, or velvet just by using your sense of touch. Most quilter's cotton fabrics are printed on a similar surface, however, which means that visual textures in a quilt must come from diversity in printed motifs. That diversity has exploded in the last few years. Those bright, tiny calicoes so prevalent in the past are still around, but to give a newer, fresher, and more sophisticated look to your quilts, there are many more medium- and large-scale patterns in "fashion" and classic colors. Fabric companies have always come out with new collections every fall and spring, but the sheer number of new designs has grown exponentially. Many of these collections are coordinated by color and scale, so combining prints within one company's line becomes foolproof. However, be brave about bringing to your mix stripes, solids, and prints from other fabric companies.

## Florals

The next time you visit a quilt shop, you'll probably discover that the number of fabrics with some type of flower printed on them is greater than any other type of print. **The sheer number of floral prints makes them an important choice for adding diversity to a quilt.** For watercolor quilts, look for medium-scale motifs in light to dark colors. For garden scenes, pick florals that are crisp and large in scale for the foreground, indistinct and small-scale for the background.

## Appliqué Bouquet

Traditional broderie perse was and still is a great way to hand appliqué lovely printed motifs onto a background. Try a quick and easy version of the technique with floral prints. **Back a printed cluster of flowers with fusible web, cut out around the blossoms and leaves (leaving no seam allowances), and arrange them so they spill out of a pieced basket.** There are no limits to the design possibilities, especially with the wide selection of pictorial printed fabrics that is available today.

## Geometric Designs

*Tip*

If you don't go for geometrics but you *love* florals, find a friend whose taste is the opposite of yours and do some fabric swapping!

Geometric prints contain repeat designs such as squares, triangles, circles, dots, or other geometric shapes. Some—like stripes, plaids, and checks—are directional. Others are printed in allover or random patterns. **The angular lines of a geometric print contrast nicely with floral prints and graceful curves.** For fabrics that can do double duty, look for geometrics that read as solid colors—their angular lines are subdued, so they provide both visual diversity *and* a calming look.

## Paisleys

Paisley fabrics still recall the distinctive, curved motifs found in woven shawls from India and Europe in past centuries. Most were large-scale prints, but today it's easy to find a wide variety of paisleys in various scales. **To make a special paisley the focal point of a quilt, try combining it with some prints in tone-on-tone and smaller-scale designs.**

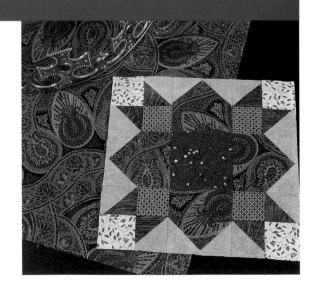

**PRINTS CHARMING**

## Reproduction Prints

**Many reproduction fabrics are close duplicates of real vintage fabrics, both in color and in motif. The fabrics featured in this block replicate fabrics made from 1860 to 1880.** Other fabrics are copies of motifs used in past centuries, but printed in modern colors. Because they come in so many types of prints and inspire feelings of nostalgia, fabrics in an old-fashioned style make great additions to your stash—even when you're not sure how you'll want to use them in the future.

## Blender Prints

**Blender prints are monochromatic, and can often appear to be sponged, painted, or spattered with irregularly shaped designs.** These prints do not depict specific objects and are also known as tone-on-tone prints. Their effect in a quilt is always the same: subtle color and texture, without a busy look.

Turn to page 74 to see how blender, or tone-on-tone, prints function as solid substitutes.

## Prints as Appliqué Backgrounds

Prints rule as backdrops for appliqué designs! Soft, muted patterns are great for creating a quiet, serene look. **Try using rich, deep, regal prints as backgrounds for contrast-color shapes.** In any case, don't settle for the first choice that works: Keep trying prints that set off your appliqué fabrics to perfection. You may go back to your first candidate, but it's just as likely you will discover something better.

## Conversation Prints

**Tip**

Next time you shop for conversation prints, take your favorite little person along and let him or her help make selections!

**Conversation prints contain small-scale designs that depict separate motifs, such as bees, pheasants, compasses, dogs, cats, rabbits, or houses.** Examples from the nineteenth century were often dark images printed on a light background. Today, these prints are just as likely to be the reverse, with lighter or more colorful images printed on a darker background. In any color combination, they make wonderful choices for a baby or child's quilt. However, even a more sophisticated project might benefit from the touches of wit and whimsy this type of fabric can provide.

## Consider Patch Size & Shape

Before cutting patches for a quilt block, think about how each fabric will appear in the finished quilt. **Large-scale prints can sometimes appear drastically different from one area to another, resulting in finished patches that look like they were cut from different fabrics.** This variety may suit your quilt design, but if it doesn't, consider isolating certain areas of a fabric before cutting out patches.

## Border Prints

**Tip**

Narrower parts of a border print are good for sashing strips that coordinate with a border cut from wider sections of the same fabric.

Border prints are complex, repeating stripes that run along the lengthwise grain of the fabric. Most border prints contain multiple, coordinating repeats in different widths. **Decorative stripes make beautiful borders for a quilt, especially when they are mitered at the corners.**

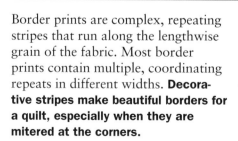

# The Quilter's
# Problem Solver

## Starting a Round Robin

| Problem | Solution |
|---|---|
| **You want to make a quilt with a group of friends. Where do you begin?** | Try some of these ideas for creating fabulous, one-of-a-kind group quilts:<br>❏ Select a colorful pictorial print, and use it as the center for a medallion quilt. Let each person who participates add a different pieced or appliquéd border in coordinating hues.<br>❏ Keep the end result in mind. If your goal is to make a certain size quilt, provide specific guidelines for everyone to follow in regard to how large or small each successive border can be.<br>❏ Create a feeling of continuity throughout the quilt. Giving each person at least one fabric that must be incorporated into her area of the quilt will produce a quilt that will be unique and well designed. |

**Skill Builder**

### Use a print fabric as a source of quilting motifs.

The next time you're stumped about just what kind of quilting design to use, try outline quilting around the shapes in a print. You can do this with hand or machine quilting. Another way to let a print guide your quilting is to quilt from the **back** of the quilt, using the lines in the **backing** fabric as your quilting design. (Before deciding on this method, make sure that your quilting stitches are as good on the reverse side as they are on the top.)

## *Try This!*

### Challenge yourself to use *only* prints in your next quilt!

Gathering together a selection of great prints for a quilt is easy:

❏ Look for fabrics that have a color or two in common, and be sure you like how the colors work together.

❏ Use different kinds of prints.

❏ Check for contrast in value between fabrics.

❏ Sort and blend fabrics on a tabletop or a design wall **before** cutting out any pieces.

With a little planning, you're sure to get beautiful results from combining prints!

**PRINTS CHARMING**

# Scrap Quilts
## *with Style*

**Q**uilters take each new piece of fabric home, knowing that someday it will be perfect for a special quilt. But when choosing fabrics for a project, what if we find it hard to put one fabric aside in favor of another? When that happens frequently, it's time to make a scrap quilt! By following the guidelines in this chapter, you'll be able to mix lots and lots of fabrics and produce quilts that are loaded with charm.

# Getting Ready

Think about what kinds of scrap quilts appeal to you most. One-patch quilts—such as the traditional Hexagon, Tumbling Blocks, and Pyramid patterns—are great because repeating a single shape is an easy and striking way to showcase a large collection of fabrics. One-patch designs are also a natural choice for making the ultimate scrap quilt—the charm quilt—where no fabric is ever used in more than one patch. There's good news, though. You don't need to have a huge fabric collection to make a wonderful scrap quilt. Plus, nearly any block pattern can be adapted into a successful scrap quilt design. Browse through quilt books for scrap quilt ideas, and don't eliminate designs that aren't scrappy. Instead, try to imagine how the blocks would look in a wider assortment of fabrics.

## Do Value Sketches

Use a pencil and ruler to draw an outline of some pattern layouts on graph paper, **or use a computer drawing program to produce designs. Make several photocopies or printouts. Experiment by filling in different areas with various shades of gray, to preview how value placement can affect the look of a design.** Don't hesitate to change value arrangements in either one-patch or repeat-block quilts—play with values until you decide on a combination of lights, mediums, and darks that pleases you. This exercise will give you a good starting point for creating scrap quilts that look evenly balanced.

## Choose Your Colors

Select a basic color combination to include in your scrap quilt. **One method that works well is to choose colors that are side by side on a color wheel, such as, yellow, green, and blue, plus the tones that fall in between these colors.**

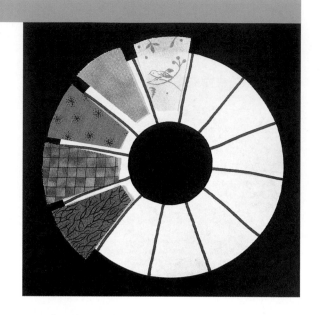

## Select Fabrics

*Tip*

Want your scrap quilt to have a country look? Avoid solids (too clean and contemporary) and large-scale prints (too elegant).

Sort through your stash, and pull out every fabric that falls within the range of colors you've chosen. **Stack colors in separate piles, taking care to include different values and types of fabric in each pile, even if they do not appear to match. Gather a mix of prints in various scales, in florals, geometrics, paisleys, dots, plaids, and other patterns.**

## Create a Color Blend

*Tip*

Sort fabrics in a well-lit room—natural light is always best for analyzing color.

**Blend your fabrics together following the order (clockwise or counterclockwise) of the color wheel.** Start with the blues, and sort them from light to dark. Then add a blue-green group, starting with dark values. Where these two groups of colors meet, the fabrics should form a subtle transition or a "bridge" that connects one color group smoothly to the next. Then proceed to the yellow-greens, beginning with lights, and continue to the yellows. Set aside any fabrics that do not fit smoothly into your blend of colors.

## Build Better Bridges

Take a close look at your blended fabrics, and then view them from a distance. Ask yourself whether they move easily from one color to another or whether there are obvious places where blending could be improved. **Try adding one or more *very* dark fabrics to dark bridges and *very* light fabrics to areas where light fabrics meet.** Not only will this help smooth out the transitions between your colors, it will give your color palette additional variety and depth.

## Find the Right Mix

When you're happy with the way your colors blend together, you can be confident that you've created a color scheme that will work well in a scrap quilt. **At this point, consider adding a few bright or bold accent colors to add zing to your design.** Also double-check for a variety of prints in different scales. Too many prints that are very similar can result in a scrap quilt lacking in visual texture. Add or subtract fabrics wherever necessary to achieve the mix you like best.

*Tip*

If transitions are still awkward, try inserting beige, brown, gray, or black fabrics as bridges between colors.

## Sort Fabrics by Value

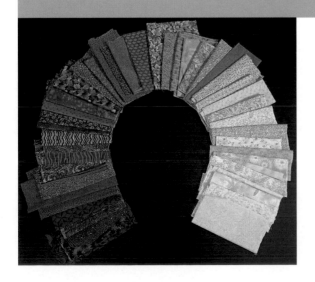

When you are satisfied with your fabric selections, forget about color completely—you have already established that the colors you've chosen will work together well. **Now sort your fabrics strictly by value, going from lightest to darkest.** Knowing how the color values of your fabrics relate to each other makes it easier for you to determine where you want to place specific fabrics in your quilt design. (For more information about value, refer to "Vary the Value" on page 38.)

SCRAP QUILTS WITH STYLE

## One-Patch Wonders

**If you're drawn to one-patch scrap quilts, cut out several patches and audition them on a design wall.** Then stand back and analyze your reaction to colors, print types, and various combinations.

## Repeat-Block Beauties

**For a repeat-block quilt, piece a few blocks and place them on a design wall, along with sashing strips and corner squares.** Switch these elements around until you're pleased with your design. Use the value sketches as suggested in the very first step of this chapter on page 89, and try some arrangements of blocks and setting pieces that correspond to these graph paper drawings or computer printouts.

## Consider Border Options

If your completed quilt top doesn't seem scrappy enough to suit you, consider adding a colorful pieced border. The traditional Flying Geese, and Diamond patterns make effective pieced borders for many scrap quilts. **Other easy pieced borders can be created from checkerboard segments or half-square triangles.** Repeat fabrics in the border that were used within the quilt to help tie the entire quilt design together. Still not scrappy enough? Highlight your quilt top with a multiborder combination!

SCRAP QUILTS WITH STYLE

# The Quilter's
# *Problem Solver*

## Sparking-Up Scrap Quilts

| Problem | Solution |
|---|---|
| **The scrap quilt you're planning on a design wall seems headed for drab results, lacking pizzazz.** | When your goal is to liven up a dull combination of colors and fabrics in a scrap quilt, try some of these ideas:<br>❑ Have you used a lot of same-value fabrics? Choose very light and very dark fabrics to add visual depth. In fact, just a sprinkling of deep, rich color can make all the difference.<br>❑ Don't use fabrics equally. There may be some you use only once, and others you repeat often.<br>❑ Use a combination of pure colors, tints, tones, and shades. A scrap quilt made only in crayon brights or only in grayed tones could be monotonous. |

**Skill Builder**

**Take advantage of these tricks for making a scrappy quilt resemble a vintage design.**

❑ Choose simple, traditional blocks.
❑ Select shirting fabrics and fabrics with small, dark, overall prints.
❑ Vary background fabrics from block to block.
❑ Alter values from block to block.
❑ Combine plaids and stripes with prints.
❑ Become familiar with fabrics that were used in the era of your choice, and simulate them in your quilt with reproduction fabrics.
❑ Although true vintage fabrics can be difficult to find—and expensive—a few antique patches here and there will add a truly special quality to any scrap quilt.

## *Try This!*

**Try overdyeing for a vintage look.** Purchase tan commercial dye in liquid or powder form. Dissolve powdered dye with a little water. Fill the washing machine with the hottest water. Add the dye and agitate briefly to mix the color. Wet up to 3 yards of unfolded fabric and add it to the washing machine. For darker color, simulating even older fabric, set the washing machine for its longest wash cycle, or repeat the wash cycle so the dye has up to 30 minutes to affect the fabric. Rinse thoroughly with cold water, until the water is clear. Dry fabric in the dryer. To keep dye from affecting future wash loads, run your washing machine immediately through a complete cycle, using hot water, detergent, and a cup of chlorine bleach.

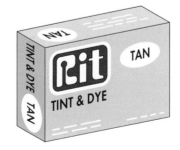

SCRAP QUILTS WITH STYLE

# Pick a Pastel
## *Palette*

I t's easy to infuse a breath of spring into your quilts with soft, dreamy colors—the hues of a snapdragon, delphinium, or jonquil. Pastels add a light, airy touch that's sure to lighten even the dreariest of winter days. Use these pale, pretty colors to create a fabric garden for yourself, a friend, or a special little member of the playpen set.

## Getting Ready

Both pieced and appliquéd pastel quilts were the rage during the 1920s and throughout the depression. In more recent times, quiltmakers have rediscovered the delicate charm of their mothers' and grandmothers' pastel quilts. Today we can choose from a wide rainbow of reproduction pastels—soft, light colors that will soften a wide variety of quilt styles. Choose a design you'd like to make in clear, light hues—classic patterns like Grandmother's Flower Garden, Dresden Plate, baskets, fans, and floral designs all work well. Pastels are perfect for recreating the look of a '20s or '30s baby quilt with appliquéd teddy bears, puppies, or kittens. Arrange a modern mosaic of small pastel squares to create a shimmering watercolor quilt.

## What You'll Need

**Various pastel print and solid fabrics**

**Muslin or other light background fabrics**

**Tissue paper in pastel colors**

**Graph paper**

**Ruler**

**Pencil**

**Colored pencils or markers**

**Sheer fabric, such as organza, chiffon, or tulle (optional)**

## Whiter Shade of Pale

Pastels are simply lighter versions of the basic colors on the color wheel. **If you've ever mixed paints, you know that adding a touch of white to a bright color creates a lighter, softer version of that hue. By this process, red becomes pink, green becomes mint, purple becomes lavender, and so on.** These lighter variations of pure colors are also called *tints*. With fabric dyes as with all pigments, the more white present in a color, the lighter the tint and the paler the pastel.

## Somewhat Darker Now

Since pastels tend to be similar in value, or degree of lightness or darkness, you'll need to be sure you select fabrics with enough contrast in value to be effective in a block or quilt pattern. Remember that value is relative—some pastels will appear lighter or darker, depending upon how you use them with other fabrics in a quilt. **Include at least one or two pastel fabrics in tints much paler than the others, and a few *comparatively* deeper, darker fabrics.**

## Backlighting

**Another way to ensure that you have enough contrast in an all-pastel quilt is to use a very light neutral as the background fabric in all of your blocks.** This may be bleached or unbleached muslin, a white-on-white print, or a subtle pale solid or print. The contrast between the background and the pastels might seem relatively low, but the pastels will still read as darker, giving your blocks visual depth.

## Complements Welcome

Pastels need not be boring. Quiltmakers—like the person who pieced this quilt top in the 1940s—often know intuitively that color complements (those colors opposite each other on the color wheel) can enliven a quilt. **Just as blue and orange are color complements, so are their pastel versions, baby blue and peach.**

## Color Illusions

Many traditional quilt blocks lend themselves to the illusion of transparency, or a see-through look. Play around with pastel-colored tissue paper to see what third color is created when two light colors overlap. Also, scout for quilt patterns (or even appliqué designs) that suggest overlapping shapes where you might use opaque pastel fabrics to simulate transparent effects. **Draw some of these blocks on graph paper, and color them in, referring to your tissue paper experiments.**

## Transparent Effects

To take the illusion of transparency into your quilt, choose fabrics with colors that match the results of your tissue paper experiments. For example, choose a pastel pink fabric and a pastel blue fabric to use in a block design made up of sections that appear to overlap. **In the overlapping area, place a lavender fabric with a slightly darker value. The result will be like looking at one pastel color through a transparent veil of the other pastel color.**

*Tip*

Secondary quilt patterns— those patterns that emerge when blocks are assembled— are often the perfect place to produce the illusion of transparency.

## Making It Glow

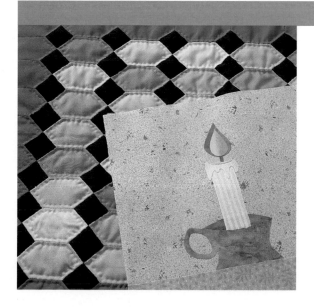

Luminous objects, like a candle flame or a blazing sun, glow from within. You can create this special effect in a quilt block through careful placement of pastels and darker fabrics. **Use a light, relatively clear color in a small area in a block. Surround it with fabrics in relatively darker, more grayed values.** The shadowy contrast enhances the look of luminosity. **Consider black or other dark fabrics for setting off the delicacy of pastels.**

PICK A PASTEL PALETTE

## Look on the Light Side

You can double the size and versatility of your fabric collection instantly by using the back, as well as the front, of your fabrics. **The reverse side of a print fabric is often lighter in value than the front, offering a more pastel version of the fabric's color or colors.** And it is usually a slightly blurred, more misty version than the front. Using the back can turn a hard-to-blend fabric into a perfect blender for a delicately colored quilt project.

## Play Misty for Me

*Tip*

For a misty patchwork quilt, layer sheer fabric over too-dark patches before assembling them into blocks or units.

**Colors of stronger intensity can often be softened to pastels by applying overlays of sheer fabric, such as organza, chiffon, or tulle.** This technique is especially effective for creating the illusion of distance, clouds, shadows, fog, or mist in landscape quilts. Overlays may be appliquéd with machine appliqué or raw-edge appliqué, or held in place with embroidery, beads, or other embellishments. When doing traditional needleturn appliqué, layer the sheer fabric on top of your regular fabric, so all the seam allowances are concealed after sewing.

## Watercolor Quilts

Soft, misty pastel fabrics are ideal for making watercolor quilts—pastels are perfect for blending and providing effective lights. **When choosing pastel fabrics for a watercolor quilt, include a range of light to pale hues. Multicolor (rather than tone-on-tone) prints in medium to large scales work best.** Avoid hard-edged geometric prints and reproduction prints that contain equal amounts of a pastel and white. Both can appear spotty and distracting, disturbing the flow of a color-washed image.

# The Quilter's
## Problem Solver

## Toning It Down

| Problem | Solution |
|---------|----------|
| **You're working with pastel, Depression-era reproduction fabrics, and the results are too busy-looking to suit you.** | Many Depression-era cotton fabrics, including feedsack prints, simply *are* busy, because they have equal amounts of white and a pastel, giving them a spotty look. To tame them:<br>❏ Add a liberal dose of muslin or another light neutral as a background fabric.<br>❏ Mix reproduction pastels with calm tone-on-tone or single-color pastel prints.<br>❏ Give the eye a visual resting place by separating busy pieced blocks with pale sashing strips, or add alternate plain blocks in period prints or pastel solids. |

**Train your eye to see pastels in unexpected places.**

Some pastel fabrics are obvious, with pink or lavender backgrounds. Others, however, are much more subtle. Remember: a pastel is simply a pure color-wheel hue that has white added to it. Sometimes tiny areas of bright color and white in combination will blend, making red read as pink, violet become lavender, and so on. Keep this in mind when selecting fabrics for your next pastel project.

## *Try This!*

**Pastel prints make wonderful baby quilts—try some of these creative ideas.**

❏ Alternate patchwork pastel blocks with plain muslin blocks. Quilt the plain blocks with colorful threads that echo the pastels in your pieced blocks.

❏ Add a touch of appliqué to a pieced pastel block.

❏ Embroider alphabet letters or nursery rhyme motifs in colorful floss on pastel blocks.

❏ Back a pastel baby quilt with a soft flannel print. Don't use muslin—it will show dirt and stain too easily!

# Dare to *Be Bold*

All modesty aside, now: It's time to take pride in your quilts, blow your own horn, and throw temperance to the wind! While you remain calm and reserved, let your quilts do the shouting. Here's to putting zip and zing in your quiltmaking, and here's how to do it.

## Getting Ready

Make it a point to go fabric shopping on a regular basis, to spark up your collection and keep it up-to-date. We owe it to ourselves to take advantage of the bounty of different prints and fabrics available to us today, and often the newest designs in quilting cottons are the most attention-getting. Notice the fabrics that jump out at you in the store, and think about how you might use them in a quilt. There really are no limits to how you can use fabrics to make your quilts livelier and full of richer visual texture.

### What You'll Need

**Assorted fabrics in a wide range of bright, bold colors and graphic prints**

**Black-and-white prints**

**Prints that combine color complements**

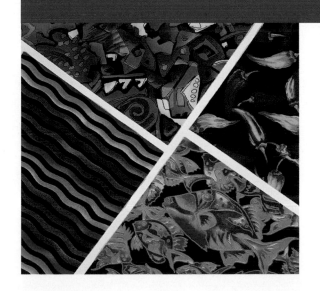

### Black in the Background

High contrast will always result in drama. **One easy way to create impact in a quilt is to use prints that have bright, eye-catching motifs against black backgrounds.** Full-strength, pure colors on a black background seem to glow or pop out at the viewer.

## Other High Contrasts

When piecing bright- and dark-colored fabrics together, try to press seam allowances toward the dark fabric, to avoid seam allowances shadowing through.

While black is often a natural choice for background fabrics because it makes colors look especially vibrant, other dark shades can also create drama in a quilt. **Consider rich coffee, charcoal gray, eggplant, or deep violet.** Use a thin, white interfacing on appliqués if the dark background threatens to show through.

## Listen to Your Fabrics

Every fabric has its own voice. When you think of the colors in a fabric as loud or soft, you're actually referring to the fabric's *tone*. What are *your* fabrics saying? For example, while subtle shades and pastels whisper softly, bright, clear, primary colors speak up with confidence. **And wild prints and neon colors—like hot pink, lime green, bright purple, or screaming orange—really make themselves heard!**

## Color Complements

Chances are that you already know the complementary colors—those colors directly opposite each other on the color wheel. **Flashes of scarlet will turn up the heat on a combination of acid yellow-greens.** When blue and orange or yellow and purple are used together, they make each other seem even more intense. Take advantage of this effect by using small doses of a color's complement.

## Look on the Bright Side

Most artists tend to think in terms of solid colors—after all, paint and paper don't come in a variety of prints! As quiltmakers, we're lucky—our medium is an almost infinite palette of *both* colors and prints. **To make a quilt dynamic, plan to incorporate some fabrics that are brighter and bolder hues than you're used to using.**

## Black & White

**For one of the most graphic effects possible, eliminate color *completely* and work with black and white alone in your quilt.** This will give even the most traditional of quilt designs a dramatic, contemporary look! Restricting yourself to these noncolors won't limit prints, patterns, or mood, and your results are bound to be powerful.

## Black, White & Bright

**Combining black-and-white fabrics with bright accent colors can result in quilts that almost vibrate with electricity.** Even if you have no confidence in your color sense, you can create stunning effects! Visit a juried quilt show and you're sure to see some attention-getting wall hangings that are black and white with touches of hot pink, lime green, brilliant orange, or cobalt blue.

**DARE TO BE BOLD**

## Bold Is Beautiful

Think about the *types* of prints you're using in your quilts. Many fabrics—like small to medium florals, calicoes, or paisleys—are fairly low-key and sedate. **To kick your fabric palette up a few notches, use larger-scale prints in bold colors and unusual motifs—think outrageous!**

## The Rainbow Connection

For an exciting color scheme, look to the rainbow—that is, an astonishingly brilliant rendition of saturated hues. **Crayon-bright colors like red, orange, yellow, green, blue, and violet, arranged in a spectrum, always manage to look fresh.** To endow these colors with some sophistication, strive for an unusual configuration of shapes rather than making a traditional quilt block.

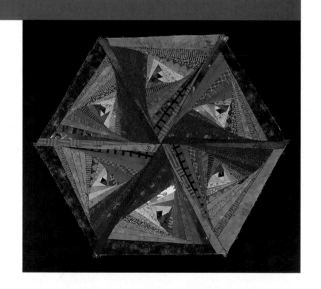

## Special Effects

**Yet another way to add more drama and impact to your quilts is to choose all kinds of exotic fabrics.** Motifs and color combinations from foreign cultures—particularly those with tropical climes—are usually full of power, energy, and heat. For more examples of special-effect fabrics and to find out how you can venture even further into the world of truly amazing fabrics, check out "Choose the Unusual" on page 26.

# The Quilter's
# Problem Solver

## From Ho-Hum to Humdinger!

| Problem | Solution |
| --- | --- |
| **Your quilt top needs something to spark it up, but you don't know what will do the trick.** | You can liven up almost any quilt design by the fabrics and patterns you choose for the borders. Think about a surround of black-and-white checkerboard. Or, why not try a brilliantly striped fabric to frame the center design? |
| **You've got the wild colors, but the quilt still looks monotonous.** | Include several shades of the same color in your design. Rather than making all of your reds a flaming lipstick shade, choose a wide range of reds, from red-orange to cherry, all the way to deep cranberry. This technique will keep the viewer's eye moving appreciatively all over the quilt surface. |

Skill Builder

### Take your cue from the fabric!

If you love safari and jungle fabrics, ethnic prints, or any kind of fabric that has representational images in it, let those shapes guide your ideas about a new quilt design. How about cutting out some zebras, giraffes, or elephants, and machine appliquéing them on blocks, lattice strips, corner squares, or borders? African mask prints can also make great sources for these kinds of appliqué shapes—use them in combination with other appliqué shapes, or mix them with traditional patchwork to add power and spirit.

## Try This!

### Give your designs a makeover with the shape of things to come.

Appliqués with fusible backings present a great opportunity to break out of the box. Avoid neat, traditional stars, isosceles triangles, parallel lines, and gentle curves. Instead, think jagged, angular, asymmetrical, and abstract. In fact, dive right in and cut shapes without marking them, then space the pieces randomly and unevenly. You'll be surprised at the impact and fun you can create.

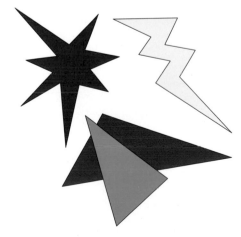

DARE TO BE BOLD

Consider the subtle shimmer of moonlight on a mountain lake, the pleasing balance of hues that marks a wild rose, the vivid display of a maple tree on an autumn afternoon. When it comes to choosing color, there is no greater inspiration or teacher for quiltmakers than Mother Nature herself.

## Getting Ready

Start your own nature-based idea file. This can be something as simple as a manila folder, a large envelope, a spiral-bound notebook, or a large cardboard box. Whatever kind of container you choose, fill it with still-life and landscape photographs, sketches, postcards, and print advertisements. Save empty seed packs and pages from garden catalogs or geographic and nature magazines. Take some time to photograph (or sketch) colors and textures you see in your own immediate surroundings, too—look closely at flowers, leaves, grass, moss, rocks, and tree bark. Take notes on the effects sunlight, fog, dew, and frost have on the different colors of a landscape. Notice how distance affects your perception of color. Tuck everything into your idea file, and refer to it whenever you want to make a quilt inspired by nature.

## Bountiful Treasures

Mother Nature's sometimes dynamic, sometimes subtle color palette offers an infinite variety of inspirational ideas. And today's fabrics make it easier than ever to recreate the beauty of nature in quilts. **In addition to traditional florals and vines, quilt-shop shelves overflow with luscious fabric prints that suggest natural textures: pebbles, rocks, and seashells, tree bark and branches.**

## Apples & Applications

Nature fabrics can be used in a variety of ways. **Fabrics that look like the sky or ocean waves are great for making quilt-block patterns like a Sailboat block.** Prints resembling rock, sand, or meadow can also help create realistic landscape quilts. **Nature prints also work well for appliqué designs—use a woodlike fabric for a tree trunk or fence, a wavy green tone-on-tone fabric for raw-edge appliqué grass.**

## Natural Teammates

**Nature prints combine nicely with other types of fabrics, as well.** The colors and textures of nature prints add a touch of unpredictability and pizzazz to florals, geometrics, paisleys, or dots, even in the most familiar quilt patterns. And because nature prints are often large in scale and somewhat abstract in design, they can take on a completely different appearance in your quilt depending on how you cut patches from them.

## Leaf Motifs & More

**While some fabrics merely suggest natural textures such as the patterns in petals, flower centers, and leaves, other fabrics literally depict motifs from nature—like bugs and butterflies.** Dense, compact pictorial motifs are great for appliqué. Cut these shapes away from their background fabrics, and appliqué them to another. Add fine-lined antennae or tendrils with embroidery or markers.

## Set the Scene

Pictorial prints may also show an entire vista, like tree-covered mountains, a tranquil seascape, or a rural meadow. **These scenic or landscape prints can add whimsy to traditional pieced blocks or become wonderful focal points for blocks that have large unpieced areas, such as an Attic Windows block.** Consider pictorial fabrics for imaginative whole-cloth quilts, too.

## Winter Wonderland

**Fabrics other than quilting cottons can produce lovely special effects in nature-inspired quilts.** Consider using overlays of organdy, batiste, or other sheer fabrics to create the illusion of fog, smoke, frost, or snow. Silks, satins, and lamés will reflect light and cause moons, streams, ponds, and snow capped mountains to shimmer. Rich velvets add depth to night skies and rose petals, while ridged corduroy can simulate wood grain or plowed fields.

*Tip*

The mottled shadings of hand-painted fabrics make them ideal for depicting skies or distant mountains.

## Natural Creativity

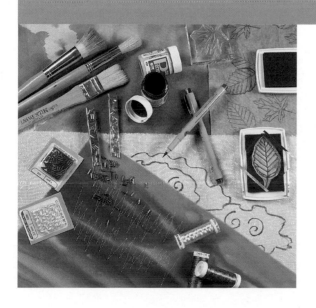

If you are unable to find the perfect commercial colors or fabrics for an inspired-by-nature quilt, consider adapting some of the fabrics you already own. The chapter, "Design Your Own Fabrics" (see page 110) suggests various techniques that use fabric paint, but don't stop there. **Consider markers, decorative threads, beads, rubber-stamping, or other embellishments.** Try over-dyeing, bleaching, photo-transfer, or any other surface design technique. Echo Mother Nature's artistry and abundance, and watch your quilt designs grow in excitement.

INSPIRED BY MOTHER NATURE

# Design
## *Your Own Fabrics*

**C**alling all arts and crafts lovers! Making your very own designs on fabric is a sure
way to guarantee that your quilt will be one of a kind. All you need are cotton
fabrics, textile paints, and a few easy-to-find supplies. From personalizing a
scrapbook quilt to making a totally unique center medallion, designing your own fabrics is
the ultimate in creative expression.

## Getting Ready

Both natural and synthetic fabrics will work for the techniques in this chapter, but 100 percent cotton looks best and handles most easily for quiltmaking. You can use white or colored fabrics, or even subtle prints. The textile paints discussed here are *not* opaque, so the color or print of your fabric *will* show through. So will underlying applications of paint, particularly if they are dark colors. Opaque paints are available, but the finished painted fabrics won't be as soft. Fabric paints like the ones in this chapter come in a starter kit of several colors, which allows you lots of opportunities for play.

Before you begin, wash your fabric in hot water with your usual detergent, and dry it on a gentle heat setting. Cut several 12-inch squares for starters. For easy cleanup afterwards, cover your work surface with plastic, or brown paper. Wear a smock or apron and put on a pair of rubber or latex gloves.

- **100% cotton fabric**
- **Rubber or latex gloves**
- **Brown paper or a plastic dropcloth**
- **Jacquard Textile Colors Starter Kit**
- **Plastic cups and spoons**
- **Precut sponge, foam, or rubber stamps**
- **Compressed sponges**
- **Colorless extender**
- **Foam brushes, 1 and 3 inches wide**
- **Iron**
- **Elmer's School Glue Gel**
- **Orvus Quilt Soap**
- **Masking tape**
- **Craft scissors**

## Mixing Colors

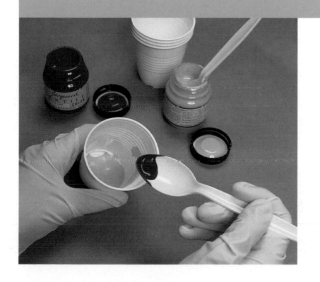

You can use textile paints directly from the jar, or blend them for a limitless palette of richer, more interesting colors. **To mix paints, start by placing a *small* amount of paint in a plastic cup (in case you end up with a color you don't like). Always start with a lighter color, and *slowly* add small amounts of a darker color to it.** For example, to produce orange, put a teaspoon of yellow in a plastic cup, and add just a little bit of red. Mix the red in thoroughly. Continue adding drops of red until you produce an orange you like.

# Stamped Designs

## Finding & Making Stamps

Scout for items that would make interesting stamps. **Many found objects work well—corks, children's tub or building blocks, scraps of wood, or even kitchen utensils.** Shapes cut from dense foam, like Plaid Enterprises' Decorator Blocks, are available at craft stores, as are compressed sponges. **Mark and cut the dry sponge.** Afterwards, run water over your cut shapes, and they'll expand in thickness so you can hold onto the edges.

*Tip*

For a color-washed background, add a little water to textile paint and brush it over your fabric square. Let it dry before stamping.

## Stamping Know-How

Use a 1-inch foam brush to apply paint to a sponge stamp. **Place the stamp painted side down on a piece of fabric. Press it firmly with your fingers, and then lift the stamp straight up.** Repeat this step as many times as you like in different areas of the fabric. **You can use the same stamp again and again in a single design, combine several stamps, or use several different colors to create your designs.** Give your imagination free rein!

*Tip*

Use colorless paint extender (see "Resources" on page 126) rather than water to thin paint. Water might make the paint runny and the images blurry.

## Dry, Wet & Overlapped Effects

Experiment! **For clear, crisp markings, apply undiluted paint to dry fabric. For blurred effects, stamp over still-wet paint or fabric that's been brushed with water.** You can even apply runny paint to the stamp, or apply different colors of paint to your stamps without rinsing off the previous color.

*Tip*

Be adventurous! Use foam brushes of any size and paint designs directly onto your fabric.

DESIGN YOUR OWN FABRICS

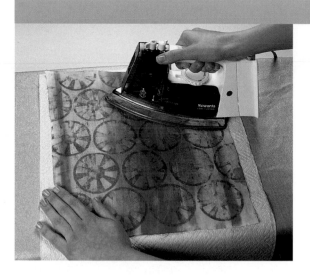

Allow the textile paint to dry completely. **Then, press the painted fabric from the reverse side for 30 seconds, using an iron at the proper heat setting for your fabric.** This will set, or bond, the colors so they won't disappear in future washings. Dry paint shouldn't stain, but do protect your ironing board cover with paper towels, just in case.

*Tip*

As an alternative to ironing, heat-set painted fabrics in your clothes dryer. Use a regular setting and put the dry fabrics in for 10 minutes.

# Masking Tape Magic

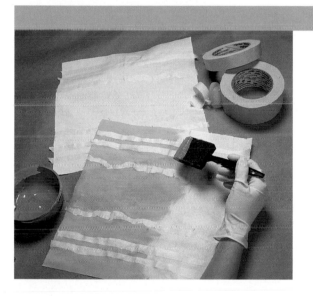

Use masking tape to make lined designs on fabric. Apply tape in various widths, in strips, squares, or even cut shapes. Wherever it is applied, the tape will prevent the paint from coloring the fabric. For a more organic look, tear strips from 2-inch-wide masking tape to create narrower strips with uneven edges. **Use a foam brush to apply a coat of textile paint, diluted with colorless extender, over your taped fabric.** If you plan on adding more paint layers, work from the lightest colors to the darkest. After each coat, allow the paint to dry completely, *without* removing the masking tape from the fabric.

*Tip*

No need to worry about being precise with masking tape—if your tape rips apart, simply tape more strips on top.

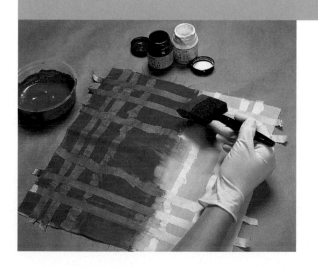

Leaving the previously placed masking tape in the same position, continue to add more strips of masking tape in different widths and in the opposite direction. **Then paint over the taped fabric as before, this time using a darker color.**

DESIGN YOUR OWN FABRICS

## Mad for Plaid

Repeat the two previous steps as many times as you like to create your own unique designs. **Perpendicular lines of tape will result in some exciting plaid or mosaic designs.** When your final application of paint is dry, remove all of the masking tape, and heat-set the paint as directed in "Get Ready—Set!" on page 113. Hand wash your finished creations with some mild Orvus Quilt Soap, to soften the fabric.

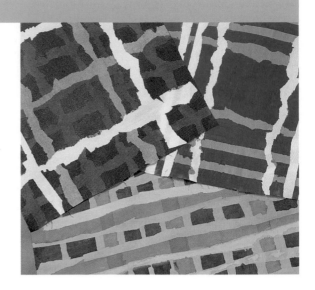

# Quick & Easy Glue Resist

## Stamp It Out!

**Tip**

Look for Elmer's (blue) School Glue Gel in supermarkets and drugstores.

Using glue as a resist will broaden your repertoire of fabric designs. Look for a washable, gelatinous glue, such as the blue-colored Elmer's School Glue Gel. Wherever this type of glue has been applied and has dried, the fabric will resist paint, just as the masking tape did in the previous technique. **Brush some glue onto a sponge stamp, and then apply the stamp to the fabric, as explained in "Stamping Know-How" on page 112, using glue rather than paint.** Allow the glue to dry completely before going on to the next step.

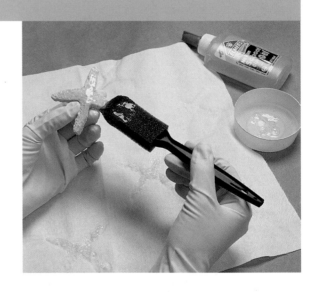

## Brush on Color

**Apply a thin layer of textile paint over the entire surface of your fabric, using a foam brush.** While the dried glue is clear, it leaves the fabric rough and slightly dimensional. Don't be afraid to paint right over glue-resist areas. This paint will come off later, along with the glue. Let the paint dry, and then set the paint, following the instructions in "Get Ready—Set!" on page 113.

## Encore!

Using the same or a different stamp, apply glue resist to some other areas of the fabric. The rough dimensionality of the dried glue applied previously allows you to space the new stamped designs around them. Let the new application of glue dry, and then **paint the fabric with a darker shade or a different, darker color, using textile paint only slightly thinned with water or colorless extender.** Again, let the paint dry completely and then set the paint with an iron following the instructions in "Get Ready—Set!" on page 113.

## Disappearing Act

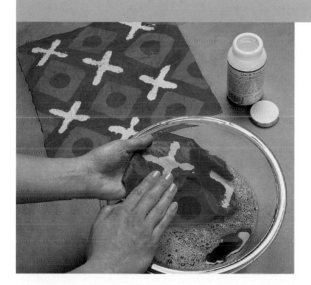

Soak the fabric in warm water for 10 to 20 minutes, to soften the glue. **Then wash and scrub the fabric by hand, in warm water, to remove all of the glue and the paint applied on top of glue. Watch the shapes of your design emerge!** A few drops of Orvus Quilt Soap will be enough to clean and soften the finished fabric.

## Glue Doodles

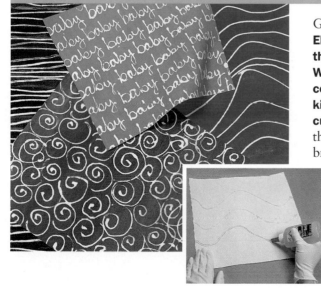

Go a little wild and crazy! **Use Elmer's School Glue Gel directly from the bottle to draw designs on fabric. With a little practice, you'll become comfortable squeezing glue into all kinds of freehand whirls, swirls, curliques, and cursive letters.** Allow the glue to dry completely. Use a brush to paint one or more colors over the surface. Follow the instructions in "Get Ready—Set!" on page 113 to set the colors. Follow the instructions in "Disappearing Act" above to remove the glue. Surprise, surprise! Look at the beautiful designs you've created!

V isual texture, a feeling of depth, a certain mood, a blending of decor, a bold statement—you can express whatever you want with the fabrics you choose. This chapter offers several versions of the same basic Square-in-a-Square block, to show you the variety of looks you can create in your projects. You'll have fun exploring the possibilities, and you'll take pride in the wonderful quilts you'll produce when you choose and use color and fabric creatively.

# Getting Ready

Page through the previous chapters, keeping in mind the kinds of quilts you like to make and your tastes in color and fabric. Now it's time to do some thinking outside the block! Do your quilts usually feature carefully coordinated color schemes? Then vary the values and animate them with accents! Is a multi-color scrap quilt with many different types of fabrics more your style? A little color planning will keep viewers gazing in admiration. Are country colors and fabrics calling your name? Try something new! Let the color and fabric combinations in this chapter inspire you to explore your own creativity.

## What You'll Need

**Your own fabric stash**

**A trip to your favorite quilt shop**

**Your imagination**

## Go for the Gold

**Create the illusion of depth in a simple patchwork block by using progressively lighter and darker tones of one color, such as with a pale yellow center that builds to a rich golden brown.** Look twice—does the center square appear to be the piece that is closest to the viewer, or the one that is farthest away?

## Let Your Lights Shine

**A glowing, clear color like "luna-moth" green is a surefire attention-grabber when combined with grayed shades of the same or similar colors.** You can make use of this luminous effect to draw a viewer's eye to specific areas or move in certain patterns across the surface of a quilt. Think of lanterns guiding you along your way. This configuration of the Square in a Square block is often called a Virginia Reel block.

## Scrap-Happy Appliqué

Think about appliqué in a new way! After piecing some traditional patchwork blocks in a selection of earthy prints to create scrappy-looking background squares, **top each block with whimsical shapes in high-contrast patterns and colors.**

## Caribbean Seas

See what you can do to create a quilt block that reflects a specific mood. Use colors and motifs that generate that mood, and patterns that contribute to the overall feeling. **For a relaxing, peaceful feeling, feature calm, cool blues and gently undulating patterns like rolling waves and related motifs, such as starfish.**

## You Oughta Be in Pictures

Capture memories in fabric—use colorful photographs that are meaningful to you, and create photo images transferred to fabric. You might let the photos function like a focus fabric, and use the colors in them to create a color scheme for a great quilt. **To honor a new baby, frame a portrait with light or bright prints, incorporating colors from the nursery or the grandparents' family room—wherever the quilt will be used or displayed.** You might even use other meaningful fabrics, such as scraps from the proud parents' wedding quilt.

**Tip**

For a family tree quilt, surround each photo transfer with leafy prints.

## Paint Your Wagon

Children's fabrics make great additions to many quilt designs. **Why not paint some one-of-a-kind juvenile prints of your own? Better yet, call on your favorite young person to help you stamp and paint some colorful and original designs on fabric.** The result will be fabulous fabrics that reflect the little artist's personality, as well as your own!

## Focus on Fun

Lighten up your quilts with a humorous print fabric. **Make reference to the name of a quilt pattern, such as Hole-in-the-Barn-Door, by featuring a farm animal figure "peering out" from the center square.** Center isolated, comical motifs within a block, and surround them with wild, rambunctious colors and patterns.

# A Color & Fabric
## *Glossary*

**Accent color.** Any color used in small amounts to spice up a quilt, usually the complement of the main color of the quilt. On the color wheel, the accent color lies directly opposite the quilt's dominant color.

**Analogous colors.** Colors that lie side by side on the color wheel.

**Backing.** Fabric used for the back of a quilt, underneath the batting layer. Quilt backings can be made from one piece of fabric or several lengths pieced together to the appropriate size.

**Bias.** The stretchy, diagonal grain of the fabric. True bias is at a 45 degree angle to the straight grain, but any off-grain cut may be referred to as a bias cut.

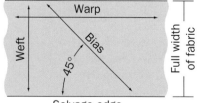

**Blenders.** Tone-on-tone fabrics that can be used to make other fabrics blend together into a more cohesive, successful color combination.

**Broadcloth.** A medium-weight fabric, 100 percent cotton.

Broadcloth is the number one choice among quilters today.

**Charm quilt.** A quilt in which no fabric is used in more than one patch.

**Chiffon.** Lightweight, drapey fabric often used in garments, sometimes also used to create special effects in quilts.

**China silk.** A finely woven, smooth silk, not necessarily from China. For quilting, it would probably be appropriate to add a light interfacing.

**Color value.** The lightness or darkness of any color, often referred to in matters of color contrast.

**Color wheel.** The spectrum of colors, commonly twelve, including primary colors (red, yellow, and blue), secondary colors (orange, green, and violet), and tertiary colors (yellow-orange, red-orange, yellow-green, blue-green, red-violet, and blue-violet).

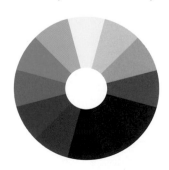

**Complementary colors.** Two colors directly opposite each other on the color wheel.

**Conversation prints.** Printed fabrics with humorous, whimsical, or comical motifs that inspire comments, laughter, and conversation related to their motifs and images.

**Cotton.** A natural fiber that comes from the boll of a cotton plant.

**Design wall.** A flat, vertical surface, usually covered with flannel, felt, or batting, where fabric combinations, patches, appliqué shapes, and quilt layouts can be easily auditioned.

**Directional fabric.** Fabric with a design that flows along specific, linear paths. Striped and plaid fabrics are the most common examples.

**Doupioni silk.** An irregular, rough, but lustrous silk fabric. The fibers are reeled from the double silk filament as it exists in the cocoon, and then spun into threads and woven into a medium-weight fabric.

**Ethnic print.** Fabrics with motifs inspired by another culture or part of the world, though usually produced domestically.

**Feedsack.** Fabric popular during the 1930s for making

sacks to hold feed, flour, and sugar. The empty bags were used for making garments and quilts.

**Felting.** Process of boiling or agitating wool fabric to shrink it and create a dense fabric.

**Fiber-reactive dye.** High-quality dye product suitable for use on fabric.

**Flannel.** Softly napped, woven fabric that is a popular choice among quilters, especially for creating a country-style look in a quilt.

**Focus fabric.** A multicolor fabric (often a floral print) that can form the basis for choosing successful color schemes for quilts.

**Freezer paper.** A roll of household paper with one wax-coated side. While designed for wrapping foods stored in the freezer, quilters iron it to fabric, since the wax causes it to adhere, and use it as template material for cutting individual patches and appliqués. Also used less frequently for foundation piecing.

**Fusible.** Describes a material that contains an adhesive activated by the heat of an iron, used to bond one fabric to another. Fusible web is backed by paper and adheres two layers of fabric together; it's popular for quick appliqué. Fusible interfacing is used to stabilize or strengthen fine fabrics or those with bias edges.

**Graph paper.** Paper marked in grid lines, used by quilters for design purposes. Grid lines

can be square, triangular, or hexagonal.

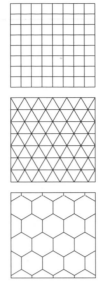

**Greige goods.** Quilting cotton fabric in an undyed, untreated state, before dyes or prints are added.

**Homespun.** Loosely woven cotton fabric, often plaid or striped; a popular choice for quilts.

**Hue.** A term that simply means *color*.

**Ikat.** A fabric made with threads that are dyed in different colors along their lengths. When woven, a regular or irregular pattern emerges in the fabric.

**Intensity.** The level of lightness or darkness of a color, affected by the amount of white or black present. The most intense colors are described as *saturated*.

**Jungle print.** Fabrics like tropical foliage, rainforest creatures, and faux animal-skin prints, usually graphically strong.

**Juvenile print.** Fabrics with childlike, often humorous motifs.

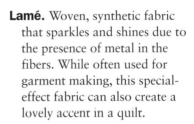

**Lamé.** Woven, synthetic fabric that sparkles and shines due to the presence of metal in the fibers. While often used for garment making, this special-effect fabric can also create a lovely accent in a quilt.

**Luminosity.** The effect of something glowing from within. This look can be simulated in fabric by surrounding a bright, saturated color with more grayed hues.

**Monochromatic color scheme.** A color combination where variations of only one color are used together.

**Muslin.** White or natural broadcloth-weight fabric, often popular for quilt backings.

**Nap.** A raised, sometimes directional surface, as found in fabrics such as flannel, velvet, or corduroy.

**Needle.** When used as a verb, the term "to needle" refers to the act of inserting a needle through the backing, batting, and top of a quilt during the quilting process.

**Neutral colors.** Noncolors that do not occur on the color-wheel, including black, white, and gray. Tans and beiges are sometimes considered neutrals.

**One-patch design.** The repetition of only one shape, such as a diamond, tumbler, clamshell, square, or hexagon, throughout a patchwork quilt.

**Organdy.** Sheer, lightweight woven fabric, sometimes used to create illusions of mist or fog in quilts.

**Pastel.** A color that contains a dose of white, producing a lighter variation of the color.

**Personal color palette.** Color preferences or choices of individual quiltmakers.

**Perspective.** A point of view, from the standpoint of a physical location. Perspective often indicates distance, whether near or far.

**Photo transfer.** Process of transferring an image from a black-and-white or color photo to a piece of fabric; a popular technique for making memory or celebration quilts.

**Pictorial print.** Printed fabrics that show recognizable, figurative motifs. Some consist of isolated motifs, while others show an entire scene.

**Plaid.** Woven, directional fabrics with sets of parallel lines that cross each other, usually at right angles.

**Primary colors.** Pure, saturated forms of red, yellow, and blue found on the color wheel.

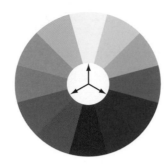

**Print.** Fabric that has a design printed on its surface, rather than woven into the threads.

**Quilting cotton.** Made of 100 percent natural cotton fibers, this fabric is the number one favorite among quilters.

**Quilt soap.** Natural cleaning solutions designed to launder quilts safely and gently.

**Reducing glass.** Looks like a magnifying glass, but images seen through a reducing glass appear farther away and smaller, not closer and larger.

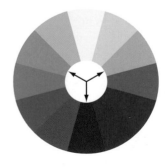

**Repeat-block design.** A quilt in which all the blocks are identical.

**Resist designs.** Designs created through the placement of glue, masking tape, or other adherents on parts of the surface of fabric to "resist" paint, dye, or other pigment. When paint is added to the fabric, these materials will keep the paint from contacting and penetrating the fabric surface. When the materials are removed, the background color is exposed to contrast with the added paint.

**Saturated.** The purest form of any color, without the presence of white or black to detract from its strength. Saturated colors are the ones found on the basic color wheel.

**Scale.** The size of designs, lines, or motifs in a print or directional fabric.

**Scrap quilt.** A quilt made from many different fabrics, usually with an informal effect.

**Secondary colors.** Colors that result from mixing together two of the primary colors (red, yellow, and blue), resulting in orange, green, and violet.

**Selvage.** Strong, tightly woven edge of fabric that runs lengthwise along both sides of the fabric. Selvages should be trimmed away and not used in quiltmaking. See the illustration on page 120.

**Shade.** A term that refers to a darker form of a color, an effect produced by adding black to the color.

**Silk.** Soft, natural fiber produced by larvae of silkworm caterpillars when forming a cocoon. Immersing the cocoon in warm water separates the silk filaments, which manufacturers reel off, spin into thread, and weave into fabric. The smoothest and costliest silk fabrics are made using long, continuous strands from cocoons that are treated before the moth has chewed a hole from which to emerge from the cocoon, resulting in shorter filaments. Many silk fabrics feature nubs and slubs where these shorter strands are twisted and joined. Silk fibers absorb dye very well, and for that reason, silk fabrics often showcase very intense colors.

**Solids.** Fabics that contain only one color and no printed pattern.

**Solid substitutes.** Fabrics that "read" as solids when viewed from a distance; these can be tone-on-tone prints or hand-dyed fabrics that actually contain a blended mix of colors.

**Striped fabric.** A directional fabric with lines running parallel to each other, usually but not necessarily along the lengthwise grain of the fabric.

**Synthetic blends.** Fabrics that contain a mix of both natural and man-made fibers, such as Polyester-cotton or Dacron-cotton fabrics.

**Temperature.** Indicates whether a color is from the warm (red,

yellow, and orange) or cool (green, blue, and violet) side of the color wheel.

**Template.** An exact copy of a pattern piece constructed from a sturdy material, like template plastic, so it can be traced around many times onto fabric without distorting its shape. While commonly used for patchwork, templates can also be used for marking appliqués and quilting designs.

**Tertiary colors.** Colors that result from mixing together a primary color and an adjacent secondary color on the color wheel. These colors include yellow-orange, red-orange, yellow-green, blue-green, red-violet, and blue-violet. Also known as intermediate colors.

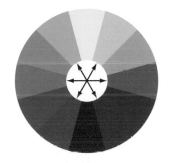

**Thread count.** The number of threads that lie in each direction in one square inch of fabric.

**Tint.** The color that results from adding white to a pure color; in fabric, tints are light, usually pastel colors.

**Tone.** The relative value of any color; shades and tints are both tones.

**Tone-on-tone print.** Fabrics that contain two values of the same color and often read visually as solid colors, especially from a distance.

**Tulle.** Often thought of as the fabric of choice for bridal veils, this lightweight, see-through, nettinglike fabric can also highlight portions of a quilt design.

**Transparency.** In quilting, a fool-the-eye effect of light seeming to come through opaque fabrics, as if they were sheer. When one fabric appears to overlap another, each seems to combine to produce a third fabric in the overlapped area.

**Ultrasuede.** Trademarked name for a nonwoven, synthetic fabric that has the look and feel of natural suede. Available in a wide array of colors, this washable fabric is useful and versatile because its edges do not fray or ravel.

**Value finder.** A small piece of transparent plastic or acrylic, tinted a color—usually red. When held up to one's eyes, the value finder makes everything viewed look to be the same color, i.e., red. Without different colors to contrast, the viewer is better able to judge the relative lightness and darkness of adjacent fabrics or items. (See "Resources" on page 126 for ordering information.)

**Vinyl.** Synthetic fabric with a rubbery, nonwoven surface.

**Warp.** Threads running along the lengthwise grain of fabric (parallel to selvage edges). See the illustration on page 120.

**Weft.** Threads running along the crosswise grain of fabric (perpendicular to selvage edges). See the illustration on page 120.

**Wool.** Natural fibers spun from the fleece of sheep.

**Judy Doenias** has been involved in crafts of one kind or another since childhood, but her introduction to quilting was a pivotal point in her life. She teaches in quilt shops and in adult education programs in New York City, and was an instructor of quilting for the Institute at the Museum of American Folk Art, where she also assisted in coordinating The Great American Quilt Festival. As vice president and later president of The Empire Quilters, she organized the members into teams to teach quilting to homeless women at three shelters in the city. She has lectured and conducted workshops for guilds and other quilting groups, assisted first and second graders in making group quilts, and has had articles about her work published in several books and magazines. She is a member of the Manhattan Quilters, a small guild of professional quiltmakers; the Online Quilters, a group that meets daily on the Internet, and is a founding member of the Quilting Judys, an international group of quilters who all share the same first name!

**Cyndi Hershey** has been a quilter since 1978, and began teaching quilting classes in the early 1980s. Her background is in interior design and textiles; colors, patterns, and textures of fabric are still the things that interest her most. Being able to combine many different fabrics in one project is the primary reason that she loves quilting. She and her husband, Jim, own The Country Quilt Shop in Montgomeryville, Pennsylvania. Her favorite part of owning the shop is that it allows her to teach as often as possible, helping other quilters learn and grow. Her class about quilting cotton, called "Cotton Tales," is always a popular one.

**Mary Anne Jordan** is an Associate Professor in the Textile Program at the University of Kansas in Lawrence, Kansas. She received a B.F.A. at the University of Michigan (1981), and an M.F.A. at Cranbrook Academy of Art (1985). Her work in surface design has been shown nationally and internationally in Japan, Poland, South America, and Canada. She has taught workshops at Arrowmont, Haystack, Splitrock, University of Iowa, and the Quilt Surface Design Symposium. Her textile art has been published in magazines and journals, such as Fiberarts and the Surface Design Journal. Her work is also included in *The Surface Designers' Art,* published by Lark Books. Mary Anne chaired the 1997 Surface Design Conference, "Material Culture," held at the University of Kansas.

**Linda Lee** is the owner of The Sewing Workshop in San Francisco, a sewing and design school for hobby and professional sewers and artists. She is also the owner of Threadwear in Topeka, Kansas, an upscale fabric store for clothing and a sewing school. As a licensed interior designer and member of ASID, she has owned Linda Lee Design Associates, an interior design firm specializing in commercial and residential design and space planning, since 1974. She is the producer of The Sewing Workshop Pattern Collection, a group of innovative sewing patterns that teach new techniques and have great style. Linda is a contributing editor of *Threads* magazine, and is the sewing expert on "Today at Home" on the Home and Garden Television Network, where she demonstrates techniques and ideas for sewing projects for home interiors. Her books include *Sewing Luxurious Pillows: A Creative Approach to Home Decor, Simply Slipcovers, Simply Pillows, Vogue & Butterick's Designer Sewing Techniques,* and *Scarves to Make.*

**Diane Rode Schneck** has been a quiltmaker since 1974 and a teacher and designer since 1980. Her first love has always been fabric. Her quilts range from updated versions of classic scrap quilts to original art quilts. Her pieces always include a wide variety of fabrics, and frequently include touches of humor. Her current concentration is on fine hand appliqué, with embroidered details and embellishments, usually focusing on everyday household objects and American pop cultural icons. Diane's quilts have been exhibited internationally and have appeared in many well-known magazines, including *Quilters Newsletter Magazine, Art I Quilt, American Quilter, Quilting Today,* and *Patchwork Quilt Tsushin,* as well as in several books. Under the pseudonym The Phabric Phantom, she began writing about fabric and fabric stores in her guild newsletter, and was the editor/publisher of *New York Unraveled!,* a newsletter about fabric shopping in New York. She is a co-founder of the popular Phabric Phantom tours, a guided adventure showing quilters and sewers first-hand where to find great fabrics in New York City.

**Susan L. Stein** began quilting in 1977 and has enjoyed the art of quilting in all of its facets ever since. She has owned two quilt shops in Minnesota, chaired a national quilt show, been state guild president, and taught locally and nationally. She has designed projects for the four Singer Sewing Library quilting books and many other publications. She has written chapters for several Rodale quilting books, has had a book of her own designs published, and is currently working on a book on Double Wedding Ring quilts. Susan especially enjoys making sampler quilts with innovative settings; she loves to use contemporary embellishments. While she purchases many commercial hand-dyes, she also dyes some fabrics herself. She lives near Columbus, Ohio, where she writes, networks with other quilters by email, sells contemporary quilts, and teaches.

**Janet Armstrong–Wickell** has been quilting for many years, but it became a passion in 1989, when she discovered miniature quilts. She is the sponsor of Minifest, the only national show and seminar devoted to small quilts. For the past several years, Janet has been a freelance writer and has contributed to many books for Rodale Press, including eight titles in the Classic American Quilt Collection series. She is the author of *Quick Little Quilts* and *Quick-and-Easy Dollhouse Miniatures*. Janet lives in the mountains of western North Carolina with her husband, daughter, and a growing menagerie of animal friends.

**Darra Duffy Williamson** collected quilts long before she began making them, and still considers the nineteenth century scrap quilt one of her greatest sources of inspiration. She is the author of *Sensational Scrap Quilts*, and has written numerous magazine articles over the years, including the popular "Traditional with a Twist" series for *Quilting Today*. In 1989, she was named Quilt Teacher of the Year, and remains much in demand, both in the United States and abroad, for her informative and entertaining lectures and workshops. Her colorful, multifabric quilts are award-winners on the local, regional, and national levels, and are held in private collections throughout the U.S. and Puerto Rico. She serves as technical writer, editor, and research consultant for Rodale Inc. and Martingale & Company publications, and will soon release her second book for the American Quilter's Society. Darra lives with her two cats in the beautiful Blue Ridge Mountains of North Carolina, which provide an inspirational palette for her quilts. When not quilting, she is usually walking, doing yoga, singing in the church choir, or scheming to improve her standing in the local Fantasy Baseball League. (She is definitely *not* cooking!)

## Acknowledgments

### Quilt Artists

We gratefully thank the following quiltmakers who graciously permitted us to show their original designs as examples of the concepts described in this book:

**Christine Adams**, Nothing but a Pack of Cards/ Signs & Symbols, 1994, on page 44.

**Joy Baaklini**, detail: The Dream, 1996, on page 14.

**Francoise Barnes**, Roman Stripes, 1984, on page 13.

**Francis B. Calhoun**, Tranquility, 1998, on page 53; detail: pastel and black doll quilt, 1986, on page 97; Reflection watercolor quilt, 1994, on page 98; untitled miniature landscape, 1998, on page 106.

**Judith Doenias**, detail of Piet at Claude's Pond, 1999, on page 47; Celebration, 1997, on page 104; both © Judith Doenias.

**Barbara J. Eikmeier**, Cherries, 1998, on page 58.

**Marianne Fons**, Flower Power, 1998, quilted by Lynn Witzenburg, on page 36.

**Carol Anne Grotian**, Two Views, A.M. & P.M., 1998, on page 48.

**Mary Gay Leahy**, The Princess and the Pea, 1994 #CQ112, on page 82, kit available through The Country Quilter (See "Resources" on page 126).

**Marquerite Malowitz**, Martha's Vineyard No. 2, 1989, and the two small quilts from the Umbrella Series, 1989, on page 32; all © Marquerite Malowitz.

**Deon Marion**, Night Lights, 1997, details on pages 2–3, 116.

**Ellen M. Pahl**, Nine-Patch in Pastel and The Four-Patch Transition, 1999, on page 94. The four-patch quilt was made from a pattern in Gwen Marston's book, *Twenty Little Four-patch Quilts*, published by Dover.

**Judith J. Roche**, greens and red quilt top, 1998, on page 102.

**Diane Rode Schneck**, Spring Comes to Lee's Market, 1989, on page 38, detail on the cover; Sea Spirals, The NJ Quilt, 1994, on page 12; Sci Fi TV, 1999, on page 26; Cloth of Heaven, 1992, on page 31; Night Quilt, 1991, on page 66; Tropical Drinks, 1993, on page 100. All quilts © Diane Rode Schneck.

**Susan L. Stein**, Natural Rhythms, 1998, on page 70; Color Wheels, 1996, details on pages 4–5, 72; Amethyst, 1993, on page 73; Monet vs. Pollack, 1996, on page 72.

**Janet Wickell**, Country Roads, 1998, on page 88; Flying Geese Mini, 1998, on page 81.

## Sample Makers and Providers

Judy Doenias, Sarah S. Dunn, Barbara J. Eikmeier, Mary Anne Jordan, Eleanor Levie, Carmen Sanchez, Diane Rode Schneck, Susan L. Stein, Jane R. Townswick, Janet Wickell, and Darra Duffy Williamson. The appliqué quilt shown on page 34 was stitched by Carol Benson, using a pattern by Eleanor Burns from *Appliqué in a Day*. The plaid binding on page 81 finishes a quilt by Reneé Fallon.

We thank Judy Roche Quilts for providing the antique crazy square, circa 1890, on page 27, Ami Simms of Mallery Press for providing the photo transfers shown on page 22 (see "Resources" for Ami's Photos-to-Fabric transfer paper). The thimbles shown on page 35 are from the collection of Rita Gilson. The Schoolhouse Quilt on page 20 and the rag balls on page 23 are courtesy of Primitive Seasons (see "Resources"). The feedsacks and feedsack fabric on page 24 are from the collection of Ellen Pahl. The Amish quilts on page 73 are from the collection of Barbara and James Emmett.

## Fabrics and Supplies

Benartex, Inc.—fabrics
Cherrywood Fabrics, Inc.—hand-dyed fabrics
Clotilde—Ruby Fabric Filter and Orvus Quilt Soap
The Country Quilt Shop—miscellaneous packets, fat quarters, fat eighths, and bolts
Hoffman California–International Fabrics—fabrics
Jacquard Textile Paints—fabric paints and colorless extender
Little Bales of Cotton—cotton bolls and miniature cotton bale
Northcott Fabrics—fabrics
Olfa/O'Lipfa—rotary cutters and blades
Omnigrid, Inc.—rotary cutting mats and rulers
P&B Textiles—fabrics
Pellon—fusible web
Primrose Gradations—hand-dyed fabrics
Rose & Hubble—fabrics
Summer House Needleworks—fabrics and supplies
Warm & Natural—batting

## Resources

**Clotilde**
B3000
Louisiana, MO 63353-3000
(800) 772-2891
www.clotilde.com
*Rotary cutting supplies, Ruby Value Filter*

**The Country Quilter**
Rtes. 100/202
Somers, NY 10589
(914) 277-4820
www.countryquilter.com
*Princess and the Pea, pattern CQ112 (shown on page 82)*

**The Country Quilt Shop**
P.O. Box 828
Montgomeryville, PA
(215) 855-5554
(888) 427-6969
*Quilters's Reducing Glass, fabrics, quilting supplies*

**Little Bales of Cotton**
P.O. Box 306
4860 Old Leland Rd.
Stoneville, MS 38776
(800) 748-9112
*Cotton bolls, miniature bales*

**Mallery Press**
4206 Sheraton Drive
Flint, MI 48532-3557
(800) 278-4824
amisimms@aol.com
*Photos-to-Fabric transfer paper*

**Primitive Seasons**
123 North Main St.
Dublin, PA 18917
(215) 249-9668
*Quilts, rag balls, country-style accents*

**Ruppert, Gibbon & Spider**
P.O. Box 425
1147 Healdsburg Ave.
Healdsburg, CA 95448
Call for nearest retail or mail-order provider:
(707) 433-9577 or
(800) 442-0455
*Jacquard Textile Colors Starter Kit, the primary and secondary color set, containing yellow, true red, orange, sapphire blue, emerald green, violet, black and white; Jacquard Colorless Extender*

**Skydyes**
83 Richmond Lane
West Hartford, CT 06117
(203) 232-1429
*Hand-painted, one-of-a-kind fabrics*

**The Summer House Needleworks**
6375 Oley Turnpike Rd.
Oley, PA 19547
(610) 689-9075
*Fabrics, quiltmaking supplies*

# Index

# Quilting Styles

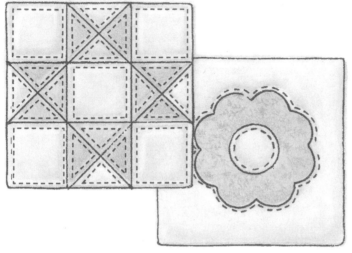

Outline Quilting

Echo Quilting

Single

Double

Crosshatch or Grid Quilting

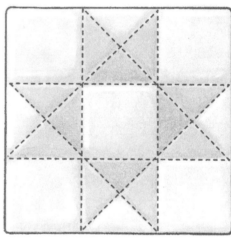

In the Ditch Quilting

Stipple Quilting

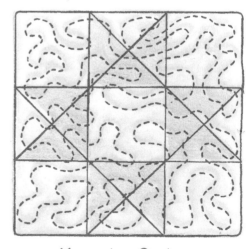

Meander Quilting